Cecil Byrd's hut. Jessie would have lived in a similar hut
during her life in Widden Valley. Both huts were destroyed in
subsequent bush fires. Photo courtesy of Greg Powell

OUT OF THE
MISTS

THE HIDDEN HISTORY OF
ELIZABETH JESSIE HICKMAN

DI MOORE

BALBOA.
PRESS

A DIVISION OF HAY HOUSE

Balboa Press books may be ordered through booksellers or by contacting:

Balboa Press
A Division of Hay House
1663 Liberty Drive
Bloomington, IN 47403
www.balboapress.com.au
1 (877) 407-4847

Front cover photo by Paul Denham

Printed in the United States of America.

ISBN: 978-1-4525-1248-8 (sc)
ISBN: 978-1-4525-1249-5 (e)

Balboa Press rev. date: 07/11/2014

CONTENTS

LIST OF ILLUSTRATIONS

AUTHOR'S NOTE

I had reached the ripe old age of sixty seven firmly believing that Glen Christina Pryor (nee Christina Margaret Nicol) was my biological grandmother. It was not until John Rayner, Glen's nephew, sought me out to tell me the truth about my father's birth that I actually heard of the existence of Jessie Hickman and Ben Hickman. They were the birth parents of my father – not Glen and her husband, Arundel!

At first I did not know what to believe. I found it difficult to believe what John had told me even though his story did answer quite a few questions that had puzzled me since childhood. Did I want to pursue the matter and find out the truth? You betcher I did! But how to research the tale I had been told? Here I was, a raw beginner, plunging into the world of family research. The first thing I had to do was to discover how to get a copy of my father's birth certificate. While I awaited the arrival of this, I read Pat Studdy-Clift's *The Lady Bushranger*. The irony of the fact that I grew up in Matraville, just down the road from Long Bay Gaol where Jessie had been imprisoned was not lost on me.

In reading *The Lady Bushranger* I found quite a few anomolies, particularly about my father's birth and the timing of various events. Was he really taken from his mother while she was in prison? I thought I knew his date of birth, but was he really born around 1911 as claimed by Ms Clift?

That was enough to send me off on nearly eleven years of research concerning my ancestors. What a journey that has been! But how rewarding!

That journey would never have been completed without the help of Jim McJannett who has been very generous in sharing his own research, experience and knowledge.

The greatest difficulty with writing Jessie's story has been joining the documentation of her life into a coherent narrative. Of course, no records detailing conversations, emotions, reactions etc. exist today as far as I have been able to discover, so it was necessary to use my imagination to provide these for the purpose of writing this book. Where oral history and documentation do not match I have used my deductive powers to make some sort of sense of them.

Oral history is a fertile field for clues. However, I found that these clues had to be subjected to the most stringent scrutiny before accepting or rejecting them. Jim and I have found many clues lurking coyly within some tale of Jessie's doings. To make that search even more difficult, Jessie was a great story teller and was never inhibited by a need to adhere to the truth. Tales that people have solemnly assured me were told to them by Jessie have proved to be, at best, a much distorted version of some event; at worst, a total fabrication in order to play a joke on some poor friend. Jessie could lie with the best of them!

I make no claim that this book is the absolute truth about Jessie. But it is the result of the research of two people dedicated to getting as close as possible to what really happened to Jessie, her family and her friends. Footnotes have been provided for those who wish to do some research for themselves. Perhaps they will find something I have missed. If so, please contact me. This is my grandmother and I am most anxious to learn all that I can about her.

At the time of writing, it has taken Jim and I nearly eleven years to bring Jessie out of the murky mists of poor research, faulty memories, myths, lies or distorted repetition as a tale passed from generation to generation. All of these have contributed in their own way to the confusion that surrounds the life of Jessie.

It is time now for Jessie to emerge from these mists and claim her place in the rich tapestry of Australian history.

Di Moore

FOREWORD

In the mid-1930s my parents bought a small farm on Nullo Mountain, a long twenty miles from Rylstone and sixty miles from Mudgee. A decade later, my younger brother and I would walk down the steep slopes of the mountain to visit Mr. and Mrs. George who lived in the valley below. We were always sure of a genial welcome and, best of all, a good helping of Mrs George's delicious homemade ice cream, a rare treat since we had no refrigeration in our house. While we savoured the luscious coolness of Mrs. George's ice cream and put off even thinking about the long, hot trek back up the mountain again, we listened to Charlie George's tales of the old days on the Nullo, where he had lived in a small cabin. Most exciting of all were the stories of Mrs. Hickman and her cattle rustling gang from whom Charlie George would hide as he heard them passing in the night.

Mrs. Hickman, as she was always called by those who remembered her exploits, died the year before my parents moved to the mountain, but they heard stories of her. Indeed, my father had seen her cave hideout near the top of a steep ravine about three miles from our house. He reported that it contained an old iron bed and three pots of homemade jam. We children imagined the dread sound of horses passing in the night, the crack of broken twigs, the rustling of branches as they pushed through the dense forest undergrowth, and shivered at the thought of the nights she had spent in that cave, for winters on the mountain featured snow, sleet and hard white frosts. Then, we thought, if she was hiding from the police, she would not have been able to light a fire for fear the smoke would draw attention to her cave.

When my father became too ill to manage the farm in 1950, we moved away from our home on the mountain temporarily, and it was many years before I was to return. But the tales of Mrs. Hickman and images of that cave with its pots of homemade jam, that combination of rough domesticity and outlaw woman leader feared by men, continued to fascinate me through the years. Five years ago I was commissioned to prepare a book on Ned Kelly, claimed to be 'the last of the bushrangers'. My research on his life and activities reminded me of our deceased neighbour, Mrs Hickman, and reawakened my curiosity about her. So, since the Kelly manuscript was completed and seventy years after her death, I set about investigating her life.

The stories people remembered and had been passed on by their parents were vague and contradictory. Some said she had been married to a lawyer, others that she had murdered her husband, or been involved in other murders. Stories about long and perilous journeys she took to sell stolen cattle, and of how she had tricked the police, sometimes with the aid of Aboriginal police trackers, were repeated with appreciation. The one book that had been written about her, Pat Studdy-Clift's *The Lady Bushranger*, contained some valuable clues, including details about her early life as a circus performer and champion rodeo rider.[1] This book also summarised information gleaned from interviews with people who actually met her in their childhood, but the myths, facts and fictions were relayed in a tangled narrative which my own family's knowledge of the history and geography of the area knew to be questionable. (Here my older brother's experience as a park ranger for the Wollemi National Park, which includes Nullo Mountain and surrounding area, was particularly important.) Newspaper reports of her arrest and trials provided some more factual (and sometimes amusing) details, which sometimes corroborated and sometimes ran counter to the stories recounted by Pat Studdy-Clift. References to Mrs Hickman on the internet tended to repeat the stories gathered in the one book.

The real breakthrough came when I discovered a short reponse by Di Moore to an account of Jessie Hickman's life by Paula Wilson in the email journal, *Bonzer*[2.] At last I felt I was touching solid ground amidst the waves of legend and beginning to catch a glimps of the true Mrs Hickman. And here was a real life connection, for Di Moore is the daughter of Jessie Hickman's son, who was given away by Jessie soon after his birth.

And now we have Di Moore's carefully researched account of her grandmother's story. It is indeed a fascinating story, but what makes the book particularly engaging is its very successful intertwining of the author's own personal discovery of her ancestry, her quest for the facts about her grandmother, her concerrn to disentangle truth from fiction and the narrative of Elizabeth Jessie Hickman's extraordinary life.

Reading the manuscript I was struck by the integrity of the author; her refusal to sentimentalise her grandmother or to be seduced by the romantic legends; her honesty about her own responses to the revelations about her ancestor and her willingness to admit the impasses she reached in her research. Here at last is a believable life of the woman whose name haunted my childhood home, a life related with objectivity, compassion and a considerable gift for involving the reader with the detective work her research entailed, as well as the remarkable story of Jessie Hickman and her family.

Lyn Innes,
Emeritus Professor of Postcolonial Literature,
University of Kent, Canterbury, England

[1]   Pat Studdy-Clift, *The Lady Bushranger, The Life of Elizabeth Jessie Hickman* (Carlisle, W A Hesperian Press 1996)
[2]   Di Moore, *Yesterday's Women, Bonzer* (e-journal) January, 2006

LIFE IN THE SADDLE

Jessie Hickman was a product of the time and place she grew up in. It was a time when travel and transport mainly depended on genuine four-legged horse power. In those days, top riders were the rule rather than the exception. To be recognised as out of the ordinary, as Jessie was, was high praise indeed.

The bulk of working horses outside cities, were grass fed, and this meant they needed spelling after periods of work to build their stamina up for another stint of hard yakka. Horses run in after a spell were usually fat, sassy and inclined to rebel against their former training by disputing their rider's right to sit astride them. Most of the battles between horse and human that have become such an integral part of our folklore, occurred not so much during the initial period of breaking-in, but when the horses came in fresh from the spelling paddocks. These impromptu displays, as well as challenge rides on known bad horses, were the forerunners of the Australian Rodeo.

Horsey minded bush girls and some city girls of the same persuasion in those times were every bit as competent astride a horse's back as their male counterparts. Just like the blokes, they would rather be rolled in the dust as many times as necessary to conquer a buckjumper than swallow their horseman's honour and ask someone else to take the rough off a fresh horse for them. This is how young Australians learned to ride.

In times prior to the 1960s, ladies' buckjumping contests were commonplace. They attracted large entries and contestants were every bit as skilled and spectacular as entrants in similar events for men.

Almost all the old time tent showmen had at least one lady in their troupe as an extra drawcard and one showman, Ken Huntly, specialised in female buckjump riders.

On reflection, it is easy to see how the Australian bush bred some of the greatest roughriders on earth. Hacking for pleasure on parkland and bridle paths can never put glue on a riders breeches the way daylight-to-dark horse work can. The instant, unthinking reflexes that hold rider and mount together in different situations can only be developed by long hours, day after day, in the saddle over all sorts of terrain.

By far the majority of great buckjump riders were battlers and the offspring of battlers. Poor people who took up or purchased properties used their children as a labour force. Boys and girls all mucked in together to assist with stock and other work. Horsemanship was a cult and a way of life to these people and while the extra physical strength of males allowed them to excel over girls at tasks like shearing, axemanship and other physically demanding jobs, it in no way impaired a female's ability on the back of a bucking horse.

Jessie Hickman, nee Hunt, became one of this country's outstanding roughriders and was regarded as the best ever by some old timers who would have been well qualified to judge. Along with her riding ability she perfected other bush skills and later became known as "The Lady Bushranger" due to her cavalier attitude regarding the ownership of stock.

She was never a bushranger in one sense of the word, having no hold-ups to her name, but for some years she did live outside the law and existed as a member of a cattle duffing gang in the Wollemi Ranges of New South Wales.

Until fairly recently, bush Australians had rather elastic morals regarding other people's stock. I personally remember a public bar conversation where two neighbouring graziers were sitting a few stools down. One grinned at the other and said "Have a beer, mate. I probably owe you one. I got a hundred of your calves last season." The man invited to drink accepted somewhat ruefully and said "You bastard! I only got eighty five of yours!"

Attitudes like this were commonplace. If Jessie Hickman dodged a few poddies, she was not alone. A lot of people were doing exactly the same thing and, be it right or wrong, in those days it was only seen as a crime if you were caught.

The Lady Bushranger was a fascinating character so please enjoy this ride in her hoof prints from the pen of her grand-daughter, Di Moore. Good on ya, Di!

Jack Drake
Horseman
Stanthorpe, Queensland

PROLOGUE

Sydney Harbour was at its scintillating best with the spring sun touching golden fingers on the waters in the wake of the ship making its way through the Sydney Heads. Not a cloud dared mar the glory of the resplendent blue sky smiling benignly on the deeper blue waters below it. Here and there various harbour craft, both large and small, puffed importantly as they went about their business. Sailing ships with their sails tidily furled could be seen as they rocked smugly at their moorings after successful – and sometimes dangerous – voyages from other lands. Around their masts ever circling-gulls screeched for scraps of food to be tossed to them.

The young man leaning on the rails of that tall-masted, white-sailed craft drank in the grandeur of the scene unfolding before him. It was not his first arrival to Sydney Harbour by any means, yet the harbour had never failed to fascinate him with its ever changing vistas. Fingers of tree-clad land reached into the harbour to point out the unfolding wonders of the gay spring flowers waving a cheery welcome to him.

His eyes searched out many of the buildings that had been built since his last visit, while he reflected that these were amazing considering the country was still in its first century of settlement. Yes, a young and vibrant land just begging for a man of his capabilities.

His mind drifted to the family he had left behind in London. Their life was squeezed into a small shop with an even smaller residence above. Similar buildings stood shoulder to shoulder in the street, looking rather like muddy soldiers on parade.

England would be slipping into her cruel winter now. The cold would be creeping into all the corners of the poorer parts of the city. People living there would be searching for anything they could use to keep that cold away. Old coats, hats, scarves – anything to keep warm. To be sure, when the snow first came it hid the ugliness of Chelsea and Whitechapel but that soon gave way to dirt, mud and slush again.

How could his father have chosen to settle there when this glorious land just begged for immigrants from its mother country, England? The young man shook his head in sheer disbelief.

Of course, his father, John Beischer, had come from a pretty cold country, being one the many Prussians who settled in London around the middle of the nineteenth century. A bread-maker by trade, he was able to make a living for himself in London. On September 1, 1859, he married Jemima Hunton in the parish of St. Lukes, Chelsea[1] where the couple went on to have a large family. Eleven children in eighteen years![2]

It was against this background of poverty, dirt and disease that the young Charles Beischer grew up. He reached the age of thirteen before he [1]managed to enter the navy as a Boy Seaman Cadet in 1875, giving his

---

[1]   Entry of Marriage (London GRO MXF 084489

[2]   Elizabeth Jemima (1860-1915) who married John Thomas Murphy; Charles Theodore (11862-1939) who married Susan Ann McIntyre (Susannah) in Australia in 1888; Lydia (1864-1865); Ann Catherine (1866-1927) who married William Henry Harbid; Clara Louise (1871-1953) who married William Thomas Pitman; Harriet Alice (1877-1925) who married William Skitmore. There are no marriage or death records which suggests that the following children emigrated to other countries (probably America); John Thomas 1867; Alice 1869; Rosina 1873; Henry Albert 1877.

age as fifteen. His reason for falsifying his age was that the Royal Navy did not accept cadets under the age of fifteen.

John died in 1878 leaving Jemima with a large family to provide for. In that same year Charles was made up to Ordinary Seaman in April, 1878.[3] Although some of the children helped Jemima it was very difficult for her to manage. Finally, she was obliged to put some of the younger children into institutions. At least Charles had found a respectable career but no record has been found which suggests he helped his mother financially.

It cannot be said that Charles' career in the Royal Navy was illustrious. During the years 1875 to 1878 his records indicates that his behaviour was acceptable. He managed to record a "Good" and even a "Very Good". After 1878 his record shows that his behaviour deteriorated showing many sojourns in the brig or in cells while on shore. Possibly his father had been a restraining influence on Charles, but with his death that restraint was gone.

While in the Navy, Charles came to Australia where he sailed in Australian waters, even going up into the islands north of there. The time that Charles served on the HMS *Diamond* and the ports to which the ship sailed are very well recorded in a wide array of Australian historical newspapers.[4] These ports include Sydney, Melbourne, Adelaide and Cossack in Australia; Auckland and Wellington in New Zealand; Fiji, Samoa, Norfolk Island, New Guinea, the Solomon Islands and the New Hebrides, which were also known as "the Cannibal Islands". In fact, Charles was in the South Seas from 18th August, 1883 to November 1, 1883.

---

[3]   Royal Navy Record 93341. The Royal Navy did not accept boys until the age of 15 so it is obvious that Charles put his age up. This is verified by him joining the Royal Navy in 1878 when he was 16 although the minimum age acceptable to the naval authorities was 18.

[4]   These papers can be found on TROVE, an internet site of the Australian National Library.

At some point in his travels he acquired a tattoo of spots on his left forearm.[5] His records indicate that he had the knack of getting into trouble as he served forty two days from the morning of April 16, 1884 to the night of May 25, 1884 in the Darlinghurst Gaol, Sydney[6], although his records do not indicate why he was there. During that year he, along with several others, deserted from the *HMS Diamond* in Melbourne, but they were all soon recaptured.[7] Charles is described in the *Victoria Police Gazette* November 19th, 1884, as 24 years old, native of London, 5 feet 7 inches tall, brown hair, hazel eyes and fresh complexion. An interesting point arises here. In the Police Gazette, Charles is described at 5 feet 7 inches, but at Darlinghurst Gaol he is described at 5 feet 9 inches. When one learns that the Royal Navy measured the men when they were barefooted and Darlinghurst Gaol took the prisoner's photo and other details while the prisoner was wearing civilian clothes and boots (possibly riding boots or thick hob-nailed boots), the answer to this anomaly becomes apparent.

When the *Diamond's* complement had completed their tour of duty, a replacement complement was sent from England. Charles and his shipmates duly returned to England on the *HMS Tamar*. His conduct in that country continued to be unsatisfactory until he was finally discharged from the navy. His records showed "Shore. Objectionable" as the reason for his discharge.[8] This term certainly approximates the modern day "Dishonourable Discharge".

---

5   Royal Navy Record 93341. It is not known when he acquired the tattoo, but it is specifically mentioned in his Naval Records.

6   Royal Navy Record 93341

7   James Melton's "Ships Deserters"

8   In those days, the captain of a ship could get permission from the Admiralty to discharge a seaman for insubordinate and worthless character describing it as "Objectionable". In Chapter 7 of "My Grandparents, John and Ellen Mills" a good description of the meaning of "Shore Objectionable" is given as "…to be paid off as objectionable character is to be ever shunned by your old shipmates as a man unworthy of being known, thus become a burden to yourself; and perhaps die at an early age, unregretted and uncared for."

The circumstances concerning the movements of Charles from England to New Zealand following his dismissal from the Royal Navy are unknown. One can only surmise. Possibly he joined the crew of some merchant ship and worked his way to New Zealand. His earlier action of desertion in Australia indicates that he was keen to settle in that land. It is most likely that he, considering his criminal record in both New South Wales and Victoria, was of the opinion that official immigration was not an option. As far as is known, he had no criminal record in New Zealand and access between New Zealand and Australia was unrestricted at that time and for many years following.

Was Charles a paying passenger from England to New Zealand? It is unlikely. His Royal Navy record contains a long list of fines. Charles would have had no – or little – money. What he did have was nearly a decade of sea experience.[9] After a time, he found his way to Australia carrying with him the mining experience he had gained in New Zealand.[10]

His original plan was to settle in The Rocks area of Sydney until he suddenly realised that most of the sailors beat a hasty track to The Rocks whenever they have leave in Sydney. If this happened, it was highly probable that one of his former mates would recognise him. That would never do!

He had to get away from the areas where ships were likely to visit. The obvious answer was to move inland away from the sea. Bathurst that was where he would go, then he would see what was the best course to take.

---

[9] It is the strong opinion of Jim McJannett that Charles signed on a merchant ship to New Zealand, deserted it at that country and, like numerous deserters, ventured to the bush where he found employment in one of the gold mines.

[10] This is supported by a letter from an American branch of the family in which it is stated that Charles went to New Zealand for a time, then moved on to Australia where it was rumoured he married. A search for further information failed to find him or his family.

It had occurred to him somewhere on his voyage to Australia that, to further conceal his true identity, it was a good idea to get a new name.[11] He settled on Hunt. A lot of people who wish to conceal their identity pick their mother's maiden name to use. This was no help to Charles until he thought to drop the "on" off Hunton, making it just Hunt. Yes, Hunt was much better! Now for the first name – he certainly was not going to use Charles! What about John? Jack Hunt? No, he did not like that one. James? Now that sounded better. Jim Hunt?

Charles sounded this name as he leaned on the ship's rail and nodded his head. He liked it. "James Hunt; Jim Hunt". It did not smack of Jack Robinson, John Smith, Bill Jones or the like, names that often attracted somewhat suspicious attention because they were so common. Also, it was not pretentious. Yes, James Hunt it would be.

Thus did James Hunt reach Australian shores around 1886 and begin his new life there.

---

[11] New Zealand Records do not reveal a Beischer entering the country and there are too many Hunts and too little individual information to be able to identify one specific person. Anyway he may not have used either Beischer or Hunt in New Zealand, which really confounds research.

CHAPTER ONE

BURRAGA

As I sit down to write this, I know that I am dying. This thing in my head is getting worse, but before it kills me I want to set the record straight about what has really happened in my life. It has been an exciting life one way and another but, because I have never hesitated to embroider the truth or even to tell a straight out lie when I was in trouble - which was often - or wanted to play a joke on someone, much of the truth has been lost. It is time now to come clean and to tell the real story - the story that has been hidden by gossip, rumours, misunderstandings and lies.

I must admit that quite a lot of these tales about me - many of them quite absurd - have been my fault. I have always found great amusement in seeing how far I can pull people's legs. Oh, just recalling some of those memories makes me smile to myself.

Without a doubt, this 'pulling someone's leg'[12] is quite a common type of humour amongst people in the bush. Having been on the receiving end of many such jokes I soon learnt just how easily fooled some people are. There are some wonderful story-tellers out there, too, but swallow their

---

[12] An Australian expression meaning to try to trick people into acting on a mistaken belief.

tales whole – I don't think so. Mart, dear Martin Breheney, would say you need a good pocketful of salt[13] when sitting around some campfires. Maybe I am not as good as some people at telling tall stories and mostly untrue, but even now I just cannot resist tempting people to their very heel ends before the bubble bursts. To be honest, some never do wake up. I cannot help chuckling at some of the things I have convinced people are really the truth.

Now I have time to sit here enjoying the sun, looking out over the peaceful paddocks towards Emu Creek and thinking about my life. I love my hut even if it does look a bit rough to other people. It certainly has very few comforts but that does not worry me. Those rose bushes I planted years ago give off such a lovely perfume and they look so beautiful against the hut, while the old peach tree bears fruit which is so sweet and flavoursome that one can make a meal out of only one of those peaches. I would like to be buried here but I suppose I will not be allowed to.

The mountains that guard the valley with their high cliffs, deep ravines and narrow tricky trails give me such a sense of security. Emu Creek grumbles along through the grassy paddocks drawing horses and cattle to it for water, while birds swoop and call to each other, either pleasingly or raucously, and I can lie here at ease and just remember!

I can see my mistakes of course - things that I could (maybe should) have done differently. Some were wrong decisions, some were the result of telling wild stories, some were simply the result of my love of the free life where there was nobody to tell me what to do. I could be my own mistress here, going and doing whatever I pleased. However, what I intend to write here will be the real story of Elizabeth Jessie Hickman, her life as best I remember it - warts and all.

As I have already said I know my time is limited. It is now March, 1936, and I am not sure I shall be here for my forty sixth birthday in

---

[13]   Be very wary of believing everything you are told.

September. This thing in my head is giving me terrible headaches and those black periods when I cannot remember what I have done may make it difficult or even impossible to finish what is really a sort of confession. If I am to write the truth in these pages there can be no self pity. What I will write may shock the reader. Many people that I know accuse me of using bad and profane language all the time. That will never do here so I promise that I will try not to use that sort of language if I can possibly help it. Still, a person cannot grow up in a travelling circus and buckjumping show without learning some very shocking - that is shocking to some - language. It sort of becomes a habit which I have found very hard to overcome.

Kitty, dear friend that she was, took me in hand for a while, trying to teach me how to speak more like she did, but it is years now since I have talked to her so I may get carried away. Please forgive me if I do.

If I manage to finish writing this, I can only hope that some kind person will get it to my brother, Hector. I would also like my son to see it and perhaps understand why I gave him away. I hope so.

I was never very interested in him when he was young because, to put it simply, I do not like children. Occasionally I will take a liking to one but that is very rare. Do I regret that past lack of interest in my son? I really don't know now, because suddenly I find I would like to see him and his family. Perhaps I should have made more of an effort when he was a baby, but I feel that I have done the right thing for him by giving him away. I do not know. It will be for you to judge. At least he has had a good life with Kitty and Arundel, a life I could never have given him.

It is hard to believe that I am a grandmother now, but the really incredible thing is I would love to hold my baby grand-daughter in my arms! I cannot explain this longing but I do realise that Kitty or Arundel may not have told my son that I am his real mother so my sudden re-appearance in his life would cause too much of an upset now that he is married and has a child of his own. Some people might feel that this unexpected yearning of mine is a sort of punishment for my treatment of Hedley. If so, there is not much I can do about it now.

I don't see why I should apologise for anything that I have done because I simply did what I had to do. Sometimes this was only to survive. Although I had some very happy times, looking back and thinking about it, it was a hard, unforgiving society that I lived in; a society that seemed determined to make me fit into the mould they saw was womanly. I had other ideas.

Now for my story.

My parents were James Hunt and Susan Ann McIntyre, better known as Jim and Susannah. I knew Mum's parents were Duncan and Matilda (nee Warren) McIntyre[14] and Mum had been born at Peelwood not far [15]from Burraga.[16] Mum told me Dad gave Robert Hunt and Mary Vidler as his parents and his place of birth as Wollongong when they got married, but she did not think Wollongong could be correct[5]. She said that if Dad was really born in Wollongong then she thought it was strange that none of the family made any effort to make the trip to Rockley for their wedding. Once when I asked her about Dad's family, she told me she had never met anyone from Dad's family. However, he did get letters from England, one even had some photos in it. Mum said Dad never read the letters to her. He would have had to do this because she could not read or write herself. She said Dad would not talk about his early life, although when he was drunk he would ramble on about his days in the Royal Navy.

Sometime in the mid-1880s Dad drifted into Burraga which was then a small mining town set in an agricultural area of the Great Dividing Range in New South Wales. Mum and Dad married at Rockley, some thirty miles from Burraga, on August 8, 1888[17]. They were very poor and, as

14   New South Wales Marriage Certificate 04019/1888
15   New South Wales Marriage Certificate 04019/1888
16   New South Wales Marriage Certificate 04019/1888
17   New South Wales Marriage Certificate 04019/1888

seems to be the way with poor folks, Mum fell pregnant immediately. My brother, Hector, was born on a property called Buckburraga, near Burraga on May 30, 1889 and Matilda McIntyre, my grandmother, was the nurse who was the midwife[18]. For some reason the names of Duncan and Kenneth were added to his registered name over the years and he became known as Duncan Hector Kenneth.

I was born in Burraga on September 6, 1890,[19] when Hector was about eighteen months old. Dad went to Carcoar, the nearest Registrar's Office, to have both our births registered. No alterations to my name crept in over the years so my legal name remained Elizabeth Jessie Hunt until I got married. Much later I was forced from time to time to use another name for a short time to avoid getting into trouble, particularly with the police. But more of that later.

Like many small country towns, Burraga had a pretty close-knit community.[20] This probably grew out of the need for people to help one another during the hard times. Burraga was awfully cold in winter with snow coming far too often, not to mention those icy cold winds that would blow in from the Snowy Mountains. The summers were probably cooler than those out on the western plains, but the winters were bitter. Anything that would help keep you warm was pressed into service. Wild animals such as rabbits were often killed for their skins, which were then tanned and often sewn into blankets or jackets or even sorts of cloaks to keep people warm. Some old bloke made a lovely rug from rabbit skins. He sort of matched the colours of the skins to make a pattern. He was so proud of it because it looked real good and kept him warm too.!

---

[18]   New South Wales Birth Certificate 17388/1889
[19]   New South Wales Birth Certificate 9828/1890
[20]   The descriptions of Burraga come from *Annals of Burraga* by Kevin Toole

R Grimshaw's Burraga Boot Palace. Mr Grimshaw seems to have a very active sense of humour as palace is hardly the word most people would apply to this edifice.

The country looked so beautiful after the snow but the beauty was hard to appreciate when all you could do was shiver. Mum said that most of the houses were poor things that were little better than canvas shelters. Looking back on those days from 1936 standards, it must have been really roughing it.

The children were able to get some sort of an education which was something. Burraga had two schools, one was a State school and the other a Catholic one. The teachers in the State school were allowed some coal to have a fire in the classroom during the winter but us poor pupils did not benefit much from it. We were left to huddle together in the classroom or to run around like lunatics to avoid chilblains or even frostbite on the really cold days.

Burraga also boasted a small hospital and a couple of general stores. Supplies were brought by wagon from Bathurst. It was pretty rough going over the tracks. You would hardly call them roads but somehow the supplies got through. There was a stage drawn by a couple of horses, but all this depended on the road being usable and not covered with water or snow, and the potholes made travel difficult. Any of these could make the carts, wagons etc. get bogged down and not get through to Burraga.

When Hector and I were old enough, Mum insisted that we go to school and learn to read and write. She could not do either and had to sign her marriage certificate with her mark which was a rather large X. She was so embarrassed by this that she was determined that Hector and I would learn to read, write and do arithmetic. It was a great handicap for Mum but I seem to remember that she did a lot of sewing for those who could afford to pay her. I know she made our clothes for us. As well, nobody ever short changed Mum because she sure knew how to count money. Poor Mum. It was such a struggle one way and another.

Burraga had two main industries, mining and farming[21]. Dad grew some potatoes at one time on land he probably rented, share-farmed or leased. As one might expect, he went bust as usual but they moved into town sometime between the births of Hector and me. The town had a copper mine and smelter and Dad was able to find work there. The miners did some pretty terrible things to the countryside particularly the rivers and creeks. For years the diggers had been washing the sludge into these waterways, destroying waterholes in the creeks and filling up the rivers. Where holes ten or twelve feet deep used to be, only sand and shingle remained by the time I was born.[22] Looking back that seems so sad.

Mum remembers when the world copper prices fell and men were put out of work and had to fend for themselves. Some tried looking for gold, usually without much luck. There was a small goldmine in Burraga too, but even for a small mine, it did not pay much.

Dad was a great story teller, often boasting about the amazing and dangerous things he had done as well as of the important people he knew or was related to. He usually found a good audience down at the pub, because the tales he told were so convincing and interesting that you could almost see yourself there in the middle of the action.

Mum said he talked a lot about his days in the navy, but he never let on if he had any family back in England. He was also quite proud of the fact that he was always in trouble with either the shore police or the officers on the ships he sailed on. He even spent some time in Darlinghurst Gaol at some stage while he was still in the Royal Navy, at least that is what Mum said.

---

[21] *Annals of Burraga* by Kevin Toole
[22] Report of T A Smith, Warden, Trunkey Division, WR 1888. See *Annals of Burraga Page 29*

Even now he is still at it, telling yarns, enthralling kids in particular, with these half truth-half fiction tales of his. Some of the stories he told children upset Mum no end because she thought that many of them were unsuitable for young ears. Looking back now, I can see how right she was. Another thing, I think he would have to be about two hundred years old by now to have done all the things he claimed to have done - one lifetime was far too short. Still, telling wild stories really didn't do much harm to anyone and he was quite popular amongst his cronies.

The real trouble with Dad was his drinking and gambling. He would bet on two raindrops running down a wall but it was all serious stuff with Dad. He also liked going for a drink - well, lots of drinks - with his mates. Never mind poor Mum stuck at home with two kids and no money. To Dad, that was Mum's problem.

Bodangora Village circa 1900

Workers at the Bodangora Mines. James Hunt is seated in the
back row near that leaning post.

In later years Mum would talk to me about Dad and the problems she had when she was with him. She said that the mines closed down when the price of copper dropped in 1891. A lot of men were laid off then and the times were very hard for Burraga folk. Dad heard that there were plenty of jobs going at the Bodangora Gold Mine near Wellington so he headed off there. Once again poor Mum was left at home with two small children to care for and no money as usual.

Dad did not get far. While he was in Bathurst he was arrested and charged with stealing clothing from Alfred Draper, John Pollard and Albert Shipley.[23] Some of the clothing was recovered, but Dad was convicted and sentenced to two years hard labour at Bathurst Gaol[24]. He came back to Burraga after that for a few years, even taking out a goldmining lease around 1896. Over the following years, he took out mining leases and operated the mines in Rockley, Burraga, Trunkey and Stuart Town[25] near Wellington. In tougher times he got work at the Bodangora Mines where he spent most of his time after Mum kicked him out. I do not think she could bear the shame of him having been in gaol.

I know we did better when he was not living with us. Mum did not get upset and angry every day because of fights over his drinking and gambling.

For myself, I do not remember all that much about Dad then, although I do have vague memories of arguments with Mum. My most vivid memory is about a puppy that Hector and I had. I cannot even remember the pup's name now, but he was just an ordinary pup that we loved - as children do[26].

---

[23] Bathurst Gaol Record 722

[24] New South Wales Police Gazette August 26, 1891 which also mentioned a tattooed cross made of spots on the prisoners left forearm.

[25] Burraga July 2, 1896; Register 11345 Series 10093 Item 7/3117 Reel 1531 Rockley January 10, 1904 Register 1617 Series 10093 Item 7/3120

[26] Jessie told this story to Wally Craven who passed it along to Jim McJannett during one of their talks about Jessie in the 1960s. As was his custom, Jim took copious notes and it is from these that the story has been taken.

Dad had this horrible tobacco pouch that was supposed to have been made from human flesh. Mum said that he had got it on one of his trips to the islands north of Australia when he was in the navy. Anyway, he was really fond of it and liked to tell all sorts of bloodthirsty stories about it. Hector and I hated it because Dad used to frighten us with the terrible tales he would tell, like how it was the skin taken off a real person and then made into a pouch. He went into the most gruesome details.

Dad would shove the dreadful thing into our faces or make us hold it while he told some dreadful tale that gave us nightmares. I think he must have hated us to do such an awful thing like that to us. What he told us was probably his imagination at work but we were just kids then. I don't know about Hector but I believed absolutely in everything he said so I was scared stiff. I was terrified that someone would cut me up to make bags. Remember he was a great story teller - even of horror stories.

Mum used to get awfully mad at him for doing this. One day she must have been really mad because she threw the pouch on the fire. It burnt to ashes but the smell in the house was something awful. Dad had come home drunk as usual and passed out. When he sobered up he demanded to know where the pouch had got to. Maybe Mum was afraid of what he would do if she told the truth so she said the pup had eaten it. Dad went crazy! Would you believe it? He shot the pup and gutted it in an effort to get the hideous pouch back! What sort of a person would do a thing like that to a puppy?

When Mum finally kicked him out for good she must have been thoroughly fed up with the way he carried on. He was little better than an animal the way he treated the three of us. Now I can only wonder that his mates at the pub put up with him.

Perhaps Mum learnt from somebody that he had recently done time in Bathurst Gaol for stealing because I doubt that he would tell her. She was a good Catholic, was Mum, and this would have been very humiliating for her. Perhaps the incident with the puppy was the last straw. Perhaps she had just had to put up with too much and could take no more of his carry on. I can only guess.

It is so long ago now I am struggling to remember exactly what did happen. All I know is that Dad was gone. The next time I can remember seeing him was well after I had joined the buckjumping show and was making money for myself. As you would expect, he only came then to bludge[27] some money from me!

Without the little money that Dad gave Mum things got really bad for us. I can remember that very clearly. Times were hard in the town and fewer people were coming to Mum to do some sewing for them so the money she earnt was less. She took in washing to make up for that, but it did not help much. It was a struggle to even get enough to eat. I expect Mum's family, the McIntyres, tried to help us, but they were a large family and they would have found it hard to make ends meet or even provide food for themselves let alone have enough left over to help us. So we went to live for a while with some of our McIntyre relaltives who were share-farming in Bankstown in Sydney. It was there that I really started to ride.[28]

The only really bright spots in our lives were the travelling shows that came to town. I loved horses - any horse was my friend. Those beautiful buckjumpers, the mine ponies or the horses in paddocks, I loved them all. The strange thing is that I think they loved me too. When the buckjumping shows arrived in town we would all go to see it. I would push my way down to the front of the crowd to get a good look at what was happening. If I was lucky, someone would lift me up onto a fence or something like that so that I could see even better. While ever there was anything to watch, I would be there watching the horses. It was so exciting!

---

[27]   Usually this means living off the immoral earnings of a woman. It is also Australian slang for persistent begging to the point where it has become most offensive.

[28]   Jim McJannet's notes on Jessie

One exciting event that happened was that Breaker Morant was living in Burraga for a while. I would sneak away to watch him ride the various horses. He was really good, too. Mum said that he drank too much, almost as much as Dad, so she did not like him much. I did not care - I was just happy to watch him on a horse.[29]

When I was about eight years old, one of these shows came to town and we all went as usual. It was Hyland's Vice-regal Circus which featured a lot of horse riding and horse tricks. You can imagine how spellbound I was by those wonderful horses and their riders. I just could not believe the things those girls could do on horseback or the tricks the horses would do like counting or even answering questions. It was pure magic for me.

When we got home Mum put us straight to bed because we were so tired. As I was going to sleep I could hear Mum crying and wondered what was the matter.

"Probably money!" I thought. Then I fell asleep.

Next morning, Mum was crying again but she dressed me in my best clothes and took me down to the show where they were all packing up. I only had eyes for those lovely horses until Mum turned me around and said, "Jessie, you are going to live with this show from now on. You love horses so you should be very happy living among so many. Just remember Hector and I love you too and will miss you dreadfully. Go on now. You belong to them."[30]

"What about you and Hector?" I cried. "Won't I be able to see you any more? I don't want to leave you! Please, Mum, let me stay! I love horses but not as much as I love you. Please let me stay! Please! Please! Please!"

---

[29] "When the Breaker went to the Boer War he would send back to the local newsagent poems and messages written on pieces of calico and old torn pieces of cloth." Letter written by Mrs Doris J Melvany. See "Annals of Burraga"

[30] It is not known whether it was Jessie's mother or father who sent her to the travelling show. Here I am assuming that it was her mother who was forced to relinquish Jessie because of her inability to support two children.

I should have known better. With tears in her eyes, Mum repeated that she loved me but said that she could not afford to keep both of us. So I just stood there, in the cold, with tears running down my face, and watched Mum and Hector walk away. Somebody took my hand and gently led me away to my new life.

The cruel fact still remains that she sent me away to a travelling show and kept Hector with her. Maybe she was hoping that Hector could get work at the mine. Who knows? But the fact remains that I was cast adrift to learn a new way of life and to fend for myself at the ripe old age of eight while Hector stayed at home. Mum said she was sorry she had to let me go, but that was just how it was in those days.[31]

I cried myself to sleep each night for weeks after that. However, when I dried my eyes and had a good look around, I found a lot to interest me and discovered that I really liked much of what I saw. As time went by I grew to like the life in a travelling show, finding many people who would tell me about their experiences with the show.[32] They also taught me how to do things like tricks in riding or training animals to do tricks.

But the horses were the main attraction and I spent as much time as I could around them. I must say that the horses helped me to settle into my new life with the show. In a way, I suppose it was only a sort of justice that Mum, Dad and Hector slipped further and further from my memory as I became more and more absorbed in my new life.[33]

---

[31] There are well documented books to support this such as Mark St. Leon's book *The Silver Road*.

[32] Research has failed to reveal who cared for Jessie once she had joined the travelling show.

[33] It is believed that Jessie went to Hyland Horse Show where trick riding was the main attraction. While her being given to Hyland's has not been documented it is known that Jessie was with Hyland's as a youngster. It is also significant that D'Arcy Hyland and James Hunt were friends. There is evidence that Jessie was only with Hyland's, Lance Scuthorp's and Martini's shows.

CHAPTER TWO

LIFE IN A CIRCUS

Once you get over the shock of being torn from your family and dumped into the hurly-burly of the daily life of a travelling circus, you find there is much to enjoy. At first, I thought I would never get used to it, but it was all so exciting and different that I found myself actually looking forward to what each day would bring. I also found that I was missing Mum and Hector less and less and making friends with others in the circus.

If I were to attempt to write in detail about those early days on the road, I would not get this all written down. It was all so exciting and new that it would take so long to tell about and I have much more important things to get on paper. Still, I did meet some great people as we travelled around so I will pick out a few and tell you about them. That way, you will understand what that life came to mean to me.[34]

The first thing I learned was the bad language everyone used – particularly the swearing and the profanity. It was impossible to be around a circus without picking up the way they talked in ordinary everyday language.

---

[34] Much of the following chapter has been culled from information contained in the books in the bibliography section of this book. Newspaper reports have also been very useful.

It is very colourful to say the least! I already knew plenty because I had heard the way miners in Burraga talked when they were drunk or looking for a fight so it was not long before I could give as good as I got if someone upset me. It must have been something special to make people laugh when a ten year old could swear like that! Oh, yes, I could swear with the best of them by the time I was ten!

I suppose it was this bad language that most of the circus people used and the dishonesty of some of them that earned us the dislike of 'respectable' people. So many people would look down on us because they thought we were thieving, immoral tramps. That was not fair because we were all tarred with the same brush, when there were really a lot of honest, hardworking people mixed in with the bad.

My next discovery was that, although circus life might look glamorous and exciting, it was also a lot of hard work – and I mean HARD work. All the animals had to be cared for so that they would perform at their best when showtime came around. This meant feeding, washing, cleaning, brushing, exercising the animals as well as lots of other jobs. As we moved from town to town tents had to be collapsed; gear packed up safely; wagons loaded and countless other small jobs done before we could get on the road. Then when we got to the next town, it all would have to be unpacked and got ready for the next show.

Us youngsters were also expected to practise each day for the acts we would be performing when we were older. These were demanding and frequently dangerous tricks and acts and many were the bruises, broken bones, cuts and abrasions that we suffered as we prepared for our future life as performers in a circus. Some never did make it to be performers, but they usually stayed on with the shows as roustabouts, riggers or labourers who were also very necessary to the well-being of a circus.

My love was the horses. This meant that at every chance I got I would sneak away to help look after them. Many a cuff on the head I got because I neglected my other chores to be with those lovely horses.

All sorts of disasters happened as we moved around. A flooded creek could cause a delay of weeks. When the creek finally did go down, we were faced with soft, sticky mud to get the wagons through. It was all hands to the wheels then – and I mean everyone – men, women and children – the lot! Then, worst of all – we had to clean ourselves up after that mud bath and boy! could that mud be damned hard to get off! The heat of summer and the cold of winter presented their own problems which we had to deal with. It was a real challenge.

As for our education, well, we just sort of picked it up as we went along. We learnt plenty about bush craft, hard work and show business, but few of us could read or write. I was grateful that Mum had insisted on Hector and I going to school and learning to do these. I helped some of my friends to read after a fashion but they usually got bored and dropped it.

In many ways, it was like living in a glass house because I saw many things that I know I was never meant to see. Things that 'respectable' people do not even know about let alone actually see. I made up my mind that some of these things were not going to happen to me so I sure learned real quickly to stand up for myself. That is why I am still quick to put up my fists (and boots sometimes) to defend myself. It also taught me that the worst thing you can do when you have to deal with a bully is to show fear. They seem to feed on fear so you have to starve them.

The other thing that girls dreaded was the grown men who came sniffing around looking for what they should not be looking for! However, that too could be dealt with. A gun kept under your pillow at night could be used to great effect when some undesirable bloke started creeping around the camp. It also helped if you did a little shooting practice so that people knew that you had a gun and could use it. I still sleep with a gun under my pillow or a rifle close to hand.

After telling you all this, I can also tell you that I was very lucky in being sent to Hyland's Horse Show because this was a family show run by

Professor Hyland and his wife. Would you believe it. They had eleven children and most of these performed in the circus.

The Hylands had travelled all over the place and it was just my luck that they happened to be near Burraga when Mum was looking for somewhere to send me. The Hylands made sure that any youngster joining their group would be looked after and clothed and fed properly. No funny business with them.

Yesterday, I dug out my tin of treasures that I keep stashed away in my secret place. It is an old Arnott's biscuit tin, one of the large ones, where I keep all my old newspaper articles, photos and other bits and pieces that I treasure now. I had enjoyed eating the contents of the tin first of course, before I started collecting treasures! Arnott's made very good biscuits which were always a treat to eat, but they also made strong tins to put those biscuits in. For people who travelled a lot, those tins made sturdy store houses for important documents and other keepsakes.

In it I found this article about Hylands which will give you some idea of what Hyland's was like. The following is only part of that article but it really describes Hylands.[35]

> *...and what a flood of recollections the circus brings up. At the sight of the white tent memories of childhood days come back to those who have long since passed the Rubicon – memories of days spent watching the preparations for the performance, of canings received for not attending school on that day, of the eager anticipation of the actual performance, and the earnest pleadings to be allowed attend. Then the evening, with its galaxy of flaring lights, and restless crowds clamouring for admittance, the open-mouthed wonder once there, and perhaps a few painful memories of cuffs received from circus hands for enjoying a surreptitious peep beneath the tent. All these memories came back last night*

---

[35]   "Wanganui Chronicle" November 26, 1903

on viewing the scene in front of the Drill Hall, where Professor Hyland has pitched his tent. There were the crowds, the lights, the tent, the piebald horses – in fact, everything we associate with the word 'circus'.

Professor Hyland has put together a talented troupe of performers, who should certainly feel flattered at the reception they received from the critical audience that assembled last evening. The acts were for the most part of the equestrian order, but variety was lent to the programme by an exhibition of wire-walking by Miss Rosie Hyland and some very clever acrobatic feats by the whole company. Mr. Tom Hyland, who is undoubtedly one of the cleverest horsemen ever seen here, showed that he was as much at home on horseback, as an ordinary person is on terra firma, and his last act – leaping on the horse from the ground while blindfolded – drew forth thunders of applause. The Misses Rose and Agnes Hyland also gave proof of their abilities as horsewomen, and performed some very difficult feats on bare-backed horses. Another equestrian worthy of note was the steeple-chasing monkey. This item caused considerable amusement. Professor Hyland is undoubtedly in his element when training horses, and the fifty odd horses which performed last night were substantial evidence of his talent in this direction.

Two of the trick horses – Sovereign and Sapphire – were really above the ordinary run of trick horses and displayed intelligence that would have done credit to many a human being. The fun was kept up throughout by the orthodox clown and dummy, but we can hardly compliment the former gentleman upon the originality of his jokes. Taken altogether, Professor Hyland provided a very acceptable evening's amusement, and thoroughly deserved the good house that greeted him.

Yep, that was Hylands all right! Someone sent me this article cut from a New Zealand newspaper but I am blowed if I can remember who it was. Of course, nobody ever wrote about the plain hard yakka required to keep such a show working. Just keeping the costumes in reasonable repair took up a lot of time. A tumble in the dirt would make it necessary for the outfit to be rinsed, if not boiled, before the next performance.

Our ordinary working clothes were nearly always messed with all sorts of nasty things which frequently gave off horrible smells. In a word, they stank! A wagon getting stuck in some mud was a sure way for someone to get a thorough mud-bath.

In my opinion it was the women who had it really tough. If they were married they had to look after their family, mend the clothing, feed the family, wash the clothes, cook and keep the camp clean. They were often called on to be responsible for the finances of the family too, which involved being able to produce the money to be able to purchase worn out clothing, boots and so on, as well as everyday things like saucepans, plates, cutlery and the like.

Oddly enough it was food that sometimes presented the most difficulty. While meat was usually fairly plentiful, it was sometimes very difficult to get vegetables. In an emergency, the women were even expected to act as doctor until reaching the next town where they hoped to find a real doctor.

At day's end they were often expected to don glamorous clothes and perform tricks that were often very dangerous and certainly tiring. As you would expect, there were many broken bones or more serious injuries sustained during those performances.

The weather sent us many challenges too. A flooded creek could hold up the whole show for weeks until the water went. Then we were often still faced with mud to get the wagons through. Added to all that was the need to keep the animals healthy and well fed!

It was the people we met that made everything so exciting. The Valdares[36] were some of the earliest ones I can remember. They were trick cyclists who worked mainly on stage rather than outdoors and I do not remember them ever performing with Martini's Buckjumpers. In Sydney, the old Tivoli and the Alhambra were more their style than a circus tent because they needed pretty solid floors for their cycles. Actually, their real names were James Mulligan[37] and his wife Elizabeth who was known as Bessie. James, who was better known as Sunny Jim, was Irish. Bessy's maiden name was Carle and they were married when Bessie was eighteen.[38] Jim and Bessy came to Australia soon after I joined Hylands, around 1899 to 1900, I seem to remember.[39]

Apart from their really clever bicycle riding they are well remembered because they trained young girls of promise to perform many of their tricks on bicycles. Julia's sister, Wilhelmina was one of these "Valdare Girls" as they became known in later years. They were much sought after by show owners. Wilhelmina went on to perform on stage as Mena Val and finally joined up with Martini's when it was formed.

After a couple of years in Australia, Jim[40] and Bessy went overseas again. I did hear that they performed in both England and France as well as America, where they performed with such well known people as W C Fields. Somewhere along the line they parted. I do not know if Bessy died or if they eventually divorced.[41] In any event, James married a Gertrude

---

36 State Library of Tasmania posters; listings of entertainers on HAT and Tasmanian newspapers January 1-7, 1900
37 Both James parents were born in Ireland; his father, Michael Mulligan and his mother, Bridget Kilkenny, migrated to America in 1865. Michael became an American citizen in Sangamon in 1868. This information has been garnered from various USA government records, census and immigration records.
38 The marriage was reported in *El Paso Daily Herald*, El Paso, Texas Saturday, July 1, 1899 where it is stated that they married in Wilkes-Barre May, 1894.
39 Notable Names in American Theatre, Necrology Section, p.475
40 Born Nebraska in 1874.
41 Bessie died in Garden Grove Retirement Home, Orange County, California in December, 1976, aged 91

Varno[42] a few years after he and Bessy left Australia. They were back in Australia around 1910 for a season before going on to New Zealand in 1911.[43] They left behind them a reputation for training first class bicycle performers.[44] I must add here that I was never one of the Valdares Girls, much as I admired how good they were. I was much more interested in riding horses than in riding bicycles.

However, I did make friends with Mena Val. That was her show name. Her real name was Wilhelmina Kelson, her parents being Lauritz (often called Fritz) and Maria Sophia. Mena really was one of the Valdares Girls but over the years she added tricks to her act such wire-walking and whip cracking.[45] At the time, it was claimed that she was the only lady whip cracker in Australia using the traditional stockwhip. She would amaze audiences by cracking a whip weighing sixteen and three quarter pounds. Another whip was said to be sixty feet long.

I would meet quite interesting people when two shows met up either out on the track or they would be in the same town at the same time. Two of these people were the Dreschler sisters, Cleo and Bonita. Cleo performed an act with pythons as well as, surprisingly, a crocodile. A real live one, too! As you probably know pythons are not poisonous. Even so, in a country where snakes and crocodiles inspire fear at the mere mention of them, this act must have had a sort of fascination of the horrible with the crowds. Cleo is supposed to have been bitten many times by snakes. She may have brought venomous snakes into her act after the time I knew

<hr/>

42 Born New York c. 1884 Father: Alexander Varno born Canada c.1856; Mother Kate Varno, born New York 1857
43 The Valdares were in Hawera, New Zealand. "Hawera Star", Christmas Week, 1910
44 Jim Mulligan died in Columbus, Ohio, on August, 16, 1962 aged 88. Bess died in Garden Grove Retirement Home, Orange County, California in December, 1976 aged 91.
45 This is the description of Mena's act as was published in "Who's Who in Wild Australia"

her. I did hear that a snake did eventually get her, in India I think it was, but I am not sure how true that is. I really do not know how she died.

Cleo's sister, Bonita, was a champion rifle shot using single bullets. She and her sister must have been really good friends, because Cleo would line up so that Bonita could shoot a sort of half-circle of disks from her head, one at a time. This was regarded as a very daring and dangerous trick. Another trick she had was to shoot her name in thirty shots in thirty seconds. Some shooting that! She would hit targets using a rifle fitted with a mirror which she held upside down, aiming at the target over her shoulder. She also did tricks while wearing a sort of Ned Kelly type mask. She never missed. In other words, she was one hell of a good shot![46]

And then there was Professor Kemp.

Well, he was a character, all right. We heard a lot of stories about him while we were sitting around a fire of an evening, relaxing after a busy and tiring day. The one that I liked best was the one about Professor Kemp and the mental asylum. Professor Kemp's real name was Patrick John Daly, but he was also known as John, Jack Daly, Paddy Daly, Paddy Kemp, Paddy Montgomery, Professor Montgomery, John Montgomery and Harry Bennett.

Jack was born at Indigo Creek in Victoria on November 25, 1870.[47] He had a brother, Richard Timothy who became a Catholic priest while Jack became a real Aussie larrikin. Richard went on to attain quite a high ranking position in the Church, but Jack got himself a gaol term. Both brothers were very clever as will be seen.

Jack was a real character who took a very casual view of the rights of ownership. You never knew what would take his eye. If that happened he would see no reason why he should not just help himself to it.

---

[46]   Who's Who in Wild Australia. Bonita was born in London in 1881.

[47]   Victorian Birth Certificate 187/21 Entry 723

He had a female roughrider called Mary Ann Gould who rode under the name of Miss Kemp. I never did hear whether they were married or not — not that it matters. Mary Ann was a top roughrider, but why she rode under the name of Miss Kemp I do not know. Perhaps she was pretending to be Jack's daughter or maybe his sister.[48]

In those days, every buckjumping show claimed that their riders were champions. The result was that there were champions running around everywhere, although there was no state or national competition to give them that title. To this day, I do not think there is a national organisation that can award the title of National Champion of Australia — either male or female.

There is a story that Jack stole a horse called Daisy Belle which was owned by a Mr. Barkley of Chiltern, Victoria, in 1899.[49] Although bush scribble and campfire tales have Mrs. Daly's Johnnie being chased by the Benalla police, there is not a scrap of proof to back this up. Jack got clean away and made a bee line for the border into New South Wales avoiding the more used roads.

He made it to Goulburn which was only a one day's ride to where his brother, now Rev. Doctor Timothy Daly, was living. The story goes that the New South Wales coppers got word of his presence in their area and went looking for him.

In the best tradition of story-telling they gave chase, until Daisy Belle turned turtle at a fence and rolled on Jack, causing quite a bit of damage to his ankle. No doubt about it. Jack could think quickly in a tight corner. When the coppers caught up with him, they found him on his hands and knees happily chewing grass. The coppers, in their wisdom, decided

---

[48] It has been claimed that Jessie rode for Jack Daly under the name of Miss Kemp. This is incorrect. It was Mary Ann Gould who did so.

[49] Kenmore Mental Hospital File SANSW NRS 17418 Con 6 Cont 312 File 512

they had a lunatic on their hands and took him back to the Goulburn Watch House.

He was then taken to Kenmore Mental Asylum on June 16, 1899, but was not accepted as the police had not filled in the paperwork correctly. At this rebuff, they took him back to the Watch House where he stayed for almost two weeks. After this time, the coppers having eventually got the paperwork done correctly, he was taken back to Kenmore.

The joke is that the staff at Kenmore were hauled over the coals, because it was considered cruel to keep an insane person in ordinary gaol cells![50]

The surprise is that, during all this, he was not charged with the theft of Daisy Belle, but with being of Unsound Mind! He was convicted of this charge and finally entered Kenmore Mental Asylum on June 29, 1899.[51]

This may sound crazy to a normal person but Jack knew what he was about. If he was convicted of horse stealing he would have gone to gaol, for him Pentridge Gaol, Coburg, Melbourne for years. Horse thieves, although they made legends of themselves, were regarded as villains by the courts and he would have been sentenced to years of imprisonment.

Jack knew that he could not be charged and imprisoned for being of unsound mind and turned that knowledge to his own advantage. His bizarre plan had worked. You cannot help loving a man that can think up such a scheme and then carry it through successfully!

To cap it all off, after Jack's ankle had healed he escaped! Kenmore officials woke up one morning in July, 1899 to find him simply gone.[52]

---

[50] Letter from the Inspector General of the Insane, Sydney, dated May 23, 1906

[51] Kenmore files contain a copy of the Goulburn Watch House sheets.

[52] Kenmore files record his disappearance.

It was not until seven years later that Jack was arrested and, at long last, charged with the theft of Daisy Belle.[53]

At some point after his arrest, when he was being sent by train to Melbourne, he jumped from the train and injured both ankles. Eventually, Jack appeared in Benalla Court on August 2, 1906, where he was convicted with the theft of Daisy Belle and sentenced to three years in Pentridge. There he remained until November 24, 1908.[54]

During much of this, Mary Ann, stood by him. He was in gaol for some three years and Mary Ann managed his show until he was released and able to look after it himself. In between brushes with the law, he had established a buckjumping show which drew great crowds to watch the various performances. Jack himself was a top roughrider, also a great teller of tales, an ability which delighted the crowds almost as much as his roughriding.

In 1905 Lance Skuthorp put a challenge in *The Queenslander*[55] for a competition to decide the Buckjumping Champion of Australia. Jack who was in North Queensland at the time took up the challenge. Mary Ann, riding as Miss Kemp, was one of the competitors. I have a photo of Mary Ann from *The Brisbane Courier*[56] which refers to her as "a champion lady buckjump rider". She was good all right, but so were other lady buckjump riders. This was a competition between two buckjumping shows and was in no way a national title.

As a sort of sideline, Jack also designed saddles which were made up by Mr. Urquhart of Bondi and sold by Walther & Stevenson Pty.Ltd. of

53   "Wodonga & Chiltern Sentinel" May 25, 1906
54   VPR 500515 V59 Prov
55   "The Queenslander" November 4, 1905
56   "The Brisbane Courier" January 26, 1906 wrote "…Miss Kemp, the champion buckjump rider, who is to appear in connection with the horsemanship competition is about 21 years of age." Mary Ann turned 21 on December 26, 1905. Jessie was only 16. The photo is not one of Jessie.

395 George Street, Sydney.[57] These saddles had a great reputation and roughriders often used them in competitions and buckjumping shows.

Sometime when I was about ten or eleven, Hylands and Lance Skuthorp's[58] shows were in town together. I knew that Lance was a tip top roughrider and sneaked away to see if I could get a look at him actually riding. No such luck, but I did manage to slip in amongst his horses. Lance had a good show so he had only the best horses and these I just had to see!

I was gently stroking a lovely chestnut's neck, when an arm went around my waist and I was scooped off my feet. The horse threw back her head and pranced in alarm.

"Better stay away from that one, girlie," a voice said in my ear. "She's doesn't like strangers and could lash out at you. We don't want you getting hurt, now, do we!" It was Lance Skuthorp himself!

"Don't be silly!" I snapped. "She won't hurt me. Look for yourself!" Talking softly and walking slowly and calmly, I approached the mare again. This time she was a bit skittish because all that sudden movement so close to her had probably frightened her. Still murmuring softly, I just stood still to let her get a good look at me and decide whether I was some sort of enemy. When she had quietened down a bit, I put my hand out for her to inspect. Keeping a wary eye on me, she inspected my hand. She accepted this so I slowly turned away from her. Nothing happened for a few moments so I guess she was making up her mind whether she liked me or not. Next thing, I felt her nuzzle my neck and I knew we were friends. I stroked her gently for a while then quietly moved away. I wish I could remember her name because she turned out to be a good horse and a good buckjumper.

---

[57]   Advertisements contained in "The Sydney Morning Herald" Wednesday, August 24, 1938 p.11 and June 8, 1938 p.12. Although this is after Jessie's death, it shows the existence of the Kemp saddle.

[58]   New South Wales Birth Certificate 16804/1870 New South Wales Death Registration 2682/1958

Lance stared at me for a while then said, "Where're you from, girlie?"

"I'm with Hylands," I replied. "Why?"

"I need an extra hand to look after the horses. I liked the way you handled that mare. You obviously know what you are doing with horses so the job is yours if you want it."

I thought for a while before answering him. Finally, I said, "To be honest with you Mr Skuthorp, I want to be a roughrider, but I do not mind mucking in with the hands to look after the horses. Would you let me ride your buckjumpers? Because if you won't I am not interested, but if you will, I am hired!"

Greatly amused, Lance threw back his head and laughed. "Got to hand it to you for cheek! How about we see what you can do before we make any decisions?"

I nodded. I knew I was good so his suggestion did not worry me at all. That job was mine! I did not expect that I would have to ride three horses but that is what happened. The first was a joey.[59] Scarcely a buck in him! The second a bit more challenging, but the third gave me a good tussle.

Jumping off the horse I walked over to Lance, slapping my hat on my leg as I went. "What's your name?" he asked.

"Jessie Hunt," I answered.

"Well, Jessie Hunt, you are certainly well named! You have more hide than Jessie, the elephant, sure enough! However, the job is yours. We will be leaving in about three days so be with us by then or the offer is gone."

"You bet, Mr. Skuthorp," I cried. "I'll be with you the day after tomorrow!"

---

[59]   In those days a 'joey' often referred to a horse in harness not pulling his weight.

I know the Hylands had been good to me, but I wanted to be a roughrider more than anything, not a trick rider. This offer from Lance was my first real break in becoming a true roughrider. I simply could not let it pass!

So I joined Skuthorp's Buckjumpers. Here I met more top people. For example, one of the first I met was to be a friend to me for almost the rest of my life and that is saying something! P. Walter Craven was his name. I never did find out what that P stood for, but I suspect it was for 'Patrick' as his father was Irish.[60] His father must have been rather like Dad and perhaps that is what made us become such good friends. Wally's mother was English and he told me that she died in India. He also had a brother but I cannot remember his name, but I do recall Wally saying he was in the NSW railways as an engineer I think.

I also learned more about Lance. He was born in Kurrajong, New South Wales, the son of a drover. His childhood was spent on the family selection in Garah, north of Moree, and he attended the Narrabri Public School. For a few years he worked with his uncle as a horseboy, but after his father left the selection, Lance became a drover. As time went by he was a horsebreaker and, later, a professional athlete. He must have been good because he came third in the hundred yard Stawell Gift race in 1894 with a handicap of eleven yards.[61]

When I joined up with Lance, the people with his show were all excited about his jump at the Blue Lake, Mount Gambier, South Australia. It appears that he repeated the jump made by Adam Lindsay Gordon[62] at the same spot years before. Now, I had never heard of this Gordon bloke but he must have been some rider! Someone threw down a challenge to Lance that he could not do the jump as well as Gordon. Needless to say, Lance could not resist the challenge.

---

60   Wally's real name was Patrick Murphy
61   Pollard Jack "The Horse Tamer" Pollard Publishing Co. 1970
62   "South Australian Register" January 20, 1886

Digging into my Arnott's tin treasure chest I found the following:[63]

> *"Our Mount Gambier correspondent telegraphed on Tuesday:-*
> *A daring attempt was made yesterday by Mr. L.A. Skuthorp*
> *(of New South Wales), to jump over the fence on the bank of the*
> *Blue Lake at the spot made famous by the leap of Adam Lindsay*
> *Gordon. The rider comes from the back blocks of New South*
> *Wales, and made the attempt with a view of sharing the fame of*
> *Gordon as a rider. Mr. Skuthorp was at first unsuccessful as the*
> *horse, the local hunter "Three Stars" could not be made to take*
> *the jump, which is really a dangerous one. He then tried another*
> *charger, but was again disappointed. The site of the jump is about*
> *250 feet south of the Gordon Monument, the fence is about 4 feet*
> *high, while on the landing side there is scarcely room to permit a*
> *horse landing. Beyond this small standing ground there is a very*
> *steep bank, leading to a precipice about 200 feet high, the deep*
> *water of the Blue Lake being immediately below. A fall over the*
> *rocks would result in certain death for man and horse. Today Mr*
> *Skuthorp made another attempt to jump the fence, and this time*
> *he was successful. He rode Mr. Boyce's hunter "Wallace" and after*
> *several attempts accomplished the feat. The fence jumped is about*
> *30 feet nearer the monument than that attempted yesterday and*
> *more dangerous. The daring rider started the horse 24 feet from*
> *the fence at a canter, taking off 4 feet from the jump. He managed*
> *to stop the horse in a single stride. About 10 feet was available for*
> *landing. The rider received a great ovation. Skuthorp expressed his*
> *intention to ride over the fence directly opposite the monument if a*
> *horse could be procured to jump at this still more dangerous spot."*

What a rider! That Adam Lindsay Gordon, too! So as far as I know, they are the only two to make that jump. Can you wonder that I hero-worshipped Lance and tried to learn all I could from him?

---

[63] "The Advertiser" South Australia October 24, 1900

Lance had his brother Cyril[64], who was always called Dick for some reason or another, to help him run the show. The two brothers contrasted the Australian style of throwing steers with the American method of bull-dogging. I have listened to many a lively discussion by people who favoured one of the two methods. Could they get wound up over it all! It was no wonder that large crowds were drawn to the performances by the competitions of horse-riding, the tales and recitations that Lance was so fond of and also the variety of the entertainment available. Lance also wrote stories and some poems. One of his better known stories is *The Champion Bullock Driver* and you will split your sides laughing when you read it.

To Dick's despair, Lance was always in debt. Sure, he made money and drew the crowds but he spent money faster than he made it. Around 1905 he was in real trouble when he bought a famous buckjumper called Snips who is reputed 'to have bucked him out of debt'. There I go, getting ahead of myself again!

It was while I was with Lance's show that I met Martin Breheney. His stage name (for want of a better name) was James Martini and when I met him he was performing as an acrobat.

---

[64] New South Wales Birth Registration 19304/1883 New South Wales Death Registration 18895.1980

CHAPTER THREE

MARTINI'S BUCKJUMPERS

When Mart joined Lance's show, Jewl was already there doing a song and dance act under the name of Miss Devine. Originally, Jewl had tried her luck with the Valdares along with her sister, Wilhelmina, whose stage name was Mena Val. Unfortunately, Jewl was not good enough to be one of the famous group known as the Valdares Girls, so she tried her luck with a song and dance routine. She had a really lovely voice which even made the crowds want to sing along with her.

At first, I was not much interested in Mart because he was an acrobat and I was only interested in the roughriders. In his turn, Mart did not take much notice of me then because I was only a kid, but sometimes he would talk to me about his travels and was always kind and thoughtful to me. Believe me, that was unusual. If a bloke was kind or thoughtful to a girl, it was frequently followed by the 'I-was-nice-to-you-now-you-be-nice-to-me' approach. Not Mart! He was different and we finally became great mates.

Although Mart did not talk much about himself, I did learn quite a bit about him as we chatted around a fire in the evenings. His real name was Martin Breheney and he had been born in Araluen in New

South Wales on 28th April, 1868[65]. His Mum and Dad were Julia and William Breheney. Mart also had two brothers, Patrick[66] and William[67], who were both born in Fryerstown in Victoria, although William's birth is actually registered in Sydney. I suppose the family moved from Fryerstown to Sydney soon after William was born. Then came Mart, followed by two sisters, Johanna[68] and Mary Jane[69], all born in Araluen.

Mart told me that he was quite young when he decided to join the circus to train as an acrobat and triple bar performer. The triple bar performers, or barrists[70] as they were often called, seem to be falling out of public favour now. Trapeze is what pleases the crowds most nowadays.

However, back then it was the skill, timing and courage required to be good on the triple bars that pleased the audiences. They appreciated just how much more demanding the skills of a triple bar performer were than those of the trapezists. The triple bar is a tremendous test of sheer brute strength, because the trapeze is not there to give the performer added momentum – momentum that helped the trapezist a lot. On the triple bar, a lack of strength or a poorly judged jump could end in broken bones, possibly putting the barrist out of work, maybe for months.

The barrist built up momentum by swinging back and forth on the first and lower bar. When he was satisfied with the momentum he had built up, he would perform at least one somersault over the higher, middle bar and catch the third bar to complete the jump. At least, that is what he

---

[65] New South Wales Birth Registration 7282/1868
[66] Victorian Birth Registration 2184/1862
[67] New South Wales Birth Registration 1788/1864
[68] New South Wales Birth Registration 7469/1870
[69] New South Wales Birth Registration 8052/1873
[70] Jack Pollard "The Horse Tamer" Pollard Publishing Co. 1970

hoped would happen. To complete a successful jump he would need to get all the strength from his arms, neck and back muscles.

It was generally thought that the triple bar was a man's act because so much strength is needed, but I have heard of a couple of girls in America who are very highly thought of. In Australia it was left to the men – if they were good enough!

Taking the stage name of James Martini, Mart performed with several partners until he joined up with Baretta and Gilbario. One must admit that Martini, Baretta and Gilbario sounds very impressive. Mart performed in both circuses and in theatres such as the Tivoli[71] and Alhambra in Sydney, but he certainly seems to have preferred the circuses as he talked about them so much. I can remember him talking about his days in *Harmston's American and Continental Cirque* that he was with around 1890. Other shows he told me about were *Abel Klaer's Circus, Kemp's show, Lance Skuthorp's show, Fillis's Circus, J C Williamson's and Harry Rickard's*. He certainly got around the travelling shows because he liked to be on the move and the roving life of such a show suited him just fine.

Mart was an acrobat who has been described as one of the greatest triple bar performers in Australia. Today, I can only say he was as good as anything I have seen.

Mart had only done a few shows with Lance when he took a tumble injuring himself to the extent that he had to rest up for quite a while. During his time with Harmstons Mart had the idea that he would like to have a buckjumping show of his own. While he was recovering from his tumble he was impressed by the large gates that Lance was getting with his buckjumpers and roughriders show. Mart wanted in on that. That really set him thinking. That was when he started planning the ways and means to make his dream come true.

It was sometime in 1900 that Mart finally decided it was time to try his luck[72]. It takes time to get a show like this together; the equipment needs to be assembled; Mart had to find riders and performers as well as hands to look after the animals and equipment. Most important of all, he had to find people who were willing to gamble on him making good.

Even before we left Lance, Mart had offered me a chance to be a female roughrider in his new venture. You can imagine how excited I was! My dream was coming true, too! Jewl also decided to come with us which pleased Mart. That was silly because what else could she have done? They were a great couple and just made for each other. Lance was one unhappy showman when he learnt that four of us were leaving to start up a new buckjumping show in competition with his! Mart, Jewl, a young bloke called Callaghan and me were the start of Martini's Buckjumpers.

Lance and Mart had never really got along well together at any time so nobody could be surprised at Lance's nose being out of joint when Mart announced he was going out on his own. And what made it worse still – in opposition to Lance. It was October, 1901 when we left Lance's show and late December, 1901 when we finally set out from Bankstown, heading up north[73].

Over the next few years we became quite a family. Mart called me "The Little Master" – not that I was very little. In fact, I was quite a tall girl even though I was only just entering my teens then. Of course, it was only a small show to start with, but Mart was sure he could build it up into something really good. He even had a special tent made for the

---

72   Jack Pollard "The Horse Tamer" Pollard Publishing Co. 1970
73   "The Argus" October, 1901

show and bought a wagon for the equipment and we set off just at the end of 1901 on our grand adventure[74]. Martini's Buckjumping Show had been born!

I suppose that at first I had a sort of image of Mart as my father because he was so much older than me, twenty two years to be exact. What I am trying to say is that there was nothing lover-like in our relationship – we were just good mates. As far as I was concerned he and Jewl were a couple even if they had not made it legal.

It was Mart's proud boast that he started out with one small tent and one small wagon but after just one tour of New South Wales and Queensland, he returned to Sydney with horses, ponies, donkeys, mules and enough equipment to load a caravan[75].

On one of his tours, he got a tip that there was a good buckjumper called Dargin's Grey, owned by a bloke called Jones[76] from the ZigZag Brewery. Mart hired the horse for one of his buckjumping events and was so impressed by the Grey's buckjumping that he eventually bought him. The good old Arnott's tin has yielded the following article.

> This is how Mart told the story[77]. *"When I left Sydney three years ago with a small side show, we just struggled along. At Parramatta the van-man thought I was going to balance him – swindle him of his money, and when I paid up he said, 'Look here, I didn't expect this. I'll tell you where there is a horse you ought to get up at Lithgow, owned by Jones of the ZigZag Brewery – that's Dargin's Grey.'*

---

74   They left the week following Christmas, 1901
75   "The Bulletin" January 4, 1906
76   John Alexander Stammers Jones
77   "The Bulletin:" January 4, 1906

Well, we went to Lithgow and I arranged to get the horse for one night for five pounds. If the chap had asked for the money in advance, we were done because I hadn't got it; but we took ten pounds and after the show I gave him his five pounds. He was so pleased that he said, "Look here, you can have the horse on Monday night for nothing.' A few days after that I bought him for eight pounds. Since then I have walked him overland right up to Port Douglas then across to Normanton. Then by sea to Thursday Island, and down to Sydney here, picking up buckers all the way."

The Grey, who was known in his early days as 'Misty", had been bred by a John (Jack) Tindall of Capertee near Lithgow then sold to a Mr. Gardiner of Wallerawang. The Grey was only a small horse[78], not much bigger than a pony when you measured him by hands[79]. He was actually broken when he was ridden bareback, but watch out if you put a saddle on him!

For some reason it was the saddle that he objected to and boy! he would put on a display of bucking that probably had never been seen before! Later, he was sold on to an Arthur Dargin and became known as Dargin's Grey[80]. The Grey was some twelve or fourteen years old when Dargin got him and he soon made a reputation for himself by throwing thirty three crack riders off his back in pretty short time. Arthur Beale described the Grey as being, a little fellow, a tad over 15 hands with the back of Samson and legs of steel!

The Grey had a really high kick which came at the end of a jarring halt, the kick ending in a wicked corkscrewing twist. In fact, after the Grey came into Mart's hands, he could only be beaten on his off days. Those

---

[78] "Warwick Examiner & Times" June 6, 1908; "Morning Post" June 2, 1903; "Townsville Daily Bulletin" August 11.1938.
[79] A "hand" was four inches high (approx. 10 cm.)
[80] "The Bulletin" January 4, 1906

off days only happened when the Grey was tired, had been on poor feed, suffered from a natural sickness or a temperament slip and at times the use of a big saddle or big steel knee pads.

The Grey had buckjumped his way through all his owners until he met up with Mart and it was Mart who made the name of Dargin's Grey famous. How Mart loved that horse! Despite being quite a small horse, the Grey was all heart and it was his determined bucking that did so much to make Martini's into one of the major buckjumping shows of that time.

Martin Breheney aka James Martini (Mart),
Acrobat and Showman

The grey had his failures too, although they were few and far between. In the issue of November 4, 1905 *The Gazette* had this to say:

> *Martini's Roughriders will give an exhibition of buckjumping and rough riding in Farlow's paddock, Windsor tonight (Saturday). All who have seen this company perform declare them to be a clever lot of horsemen, and the show to be a genuine one. There are many humorous incidents in connection with the riding of tricky mules and horses, which cause the audience to scream with laughter. Among the buckjumpers is the notorious Dargin's Grey, well known here. It will be remembered that the ill-fated Harry Morant ("The Breaker") successfully rode Dargin's Grey at the Hawkesbury show in 1901 when the animal had the reputation of having thrown all the Australian rough-riders of note. "Bobs" is another outlaw and Mr Martini is prepared to make a big wager that no rider can stay on him for five minutes. The company has over 40 horses and gives a legitimate show that anyone can attend.*

This article is near an ad in the same issue telling of our travels for two and a half years in Queensland and that we were returning now from the Gulf. According to them we had 22 buckjumpers (6 of them from Queensland although I do not know what that had to do with anything). We also had bucking horses, ponies, mules, donkeys, jeanets, and asses.

Arthur Beale said that there was many a pub and cattleyard blower that claimed to have successfully mastered the Grey but in the main they were nothing but froth and bubble. Windbags! Not a dozen out of hundreds got the better of the Capertee-bred old Arab brumby cross. And mostly, those that did were best of the best and some of them only bested the Grey when he was off-peak and not too inclined to buck.[81]

---

[81] Taken from Jim McJannett's notes of a talk with Arthur Beale, Rotorua, New Zealand, 1963.

> One of Mart's favourite stories was how the Grey broke his
> leg[82]. *"The old horse was hurt at Toowoomba and was having a*
> *spell. He had twisted himself, came down hard and smashed his*
> *rear fetlock - you could hear the crack! But he still bucked away*
> *on three legs — bucked until he threw Hunt who was riding him.*
>
> *Jack Prendergast said he believed that if the Grey was lying down*
> *on his last gasp and anybody got on him, he'd get up and buck*
> *himself to death."*

Mart nursed the Grey back to health after his accident but never allowed
anyone to ride him again. Mart simply displayed him as "The Legend
That Was". Everyone was so sad when the Grey died on January 11,
1909, near Nyngan, New South Wales at the ripe old age of twenty
nine[83].

Getting back to my story… Mart and Jewl worked very hard promoting
and managing the show and keeping the standard of entertainment up.
Jewl was very kind to me and I grew to be very fond of them both as time
went by. Jewl was only thirteen years older than me so I felt a bit as if
she were my older sister. Trust me! Just thinking about those days has
brought tears to my eyes and, believe me, I do not cry easily! Those days
had to be the happiest of my life.

As I said, Mart was different. He was kind and considerate but, more
importantly to male roughriders, he had no hesitation in letting me ride
the wildest of his horses. He knew I could ride them! It annoyed some of
the men but that never worried me. What really annoyed me was the way
the men got the big write-ups in the newspapers and advertising sheets
while I was lucky to get a mention. I knew I was as good as they were
and what is more, they jolly well knew it too! But it made no difference,
I barely rated a mention.

---

[82] "The Bulletin" January 4, 1906
[83] "The Referee" January 20, 1909

Mart was an acrobat not a roughrider but he understood what it took to be a roughrider. That really good article about Martini's in the *Bulletin*[84] shows this:

> *This last three years I have seen the best buckjumping horses and the best riders in the world and I tell you it is practice makes perfect. A little man can ride as well as a big man; you watch George Hoskins tonight. He is not a little man but not long-legged and that's what you mean. A balanced rider doesn't use his legs to grip his horse all the time; he's just moving to meet him, playing him as you might a fish; and gripping him with all his power for the moment that his grip is needed. A man ought to be able to ride a buckjumper quite well at fifty if he's a balanced rider. It doesn't do him a bit of harm because he is moving with the horse. Riding loose, you are all over the horse, one time on his back another on his rump but you're always on him. If you've got a stiff seat, once he shifts you, he shifts you for good. It's just like me handling my gymnastic bars; at one time you have to hang on with all your power, at others you are just touching lightly."*

Mart sure knew what he was talking about!

Well, that was my life during those years. I was with Mart's show right up till 1910 when it was sold. One thing that was a real problem during those years was my Dad. When we were performing anywhere near Wellington in New South Wales or somewhere he could get to fairly easily, he would turn up trying to get money from me. Dad got his come-uppance one day though[85].

Apart from these unwelcome visits from Dad, my years with Martini's were ones of pure happiness, travelling around the country, being with people I knew and liked and working hard to keep a good show up to

84 "The Bulletin" January 4, 1906
85 The story as told to Jim McJannett by Wally Craven

the mark. There seemed to be no shadows on my happiness. Nowadays, I think my idea of Heaven would be to be back in those days with Mart and Jewl, the show, the horses and the friends.

Not long before we got to Windsor in November, 1905, Mart came up with the idea of "Fun in a Stockyard"[86]. It was an instant success because it was both simple and funny. Ponies, mules and donkeys were let loose in the ring and the children in the audience invited to try to ride them. Since both children and animals are unpredictable, the result was some really funny high jinks. Of course, the clowns joined in the mayhem and the adult audience just loved it.

We toured all over the place but I particularly liked the far north of Queensland. The trees and flowers and ferns were just so beautiful, but what really fascinated me were the coconuts – they were amazing. Mart just about split his sides laughing when I tried to smash into a coconut by whacking it with a stone. When I eventually broke through the shell, I got covered in the watery stuff that came out of it. It made a mess but tasted good. I wish I could go back there now but it is too late. My memories will have to do.

1906 was a big year for the show. In January *The Bulletin* ran a long article about Mart and his show. It is far too long to copy out here but one thing worth noticing is that Mart made his famous offer of one hundred pounds if anyone could ride Bobs for five minutes[87]. Another article in *The Referee* tells how Mr. Suldy, a leading New Zealand rider, tried to ride Bobs but was thrown in seventeen seconds[88]!

Around February there were at least two big shows in Queensland – Jack Kemp's and Lance Skuthorp's[89]. It was not unusual for challenges to be

---

[86] "The Gazette" November 4, 1905

[87] "The Bulletin" January 4, 1906

[88] "The Referee" January, 1906

[89] "The Queenslander" February 3, 1906

made between shows when this happened. Sometimes more than two shows would set up a competition and it often happened that the winner of these events would claim to be Australian Champion in whatever event they won. Not true! As far as I know there is still no organisation or association who has the authority to award such a title[90]. This only applied to the professional roughriders, of course.

In most buckjumping shows the usual routine was to invite anyone from the crowd to ride one of the show's buckjumpers for a set time – if they could. Riders who fancied their chances of staying on a horse's or bullock's back would come forward and see what they could do. If they did manage to do this there was usually some cash prize for staying on the horse that long. Some horses were easily ridden and did not last long in the show; some of the would-be riders over-estimated their riding ability resulting in some pretty heavy falls or even injuries of some sort[91].

Martini's famous buckjumper 'Dargin's Grey', a small horse
who is said to have continued bucking after breaking his leg.

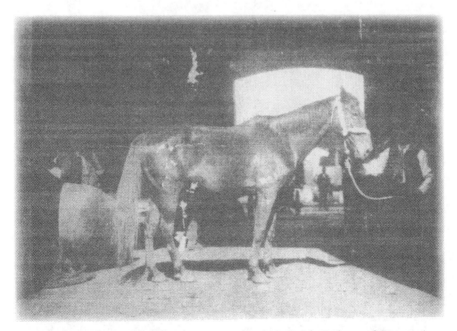

Another of Martini's buckjumpers 'Bobs'. Both Bobs and Dargin's
Grey deserve a place of honour in any Buckjumper's Hall of Fame

The big drawcard was to see if anyone could ride the show's star buckjumper. These kings of buckjumpers were hardly ever ridden by would-be roughriders, horses like Dargin's Grey and Bobs. Of course, people were invited to put their local horses into the ring to see how many riders they could toss. Mart found many a good buckjumper and roughrider amongst these amateurs.

When a show came into town, the newspapers would give it a terrific write-up. As I said earlier, it always seemed to be the men they wrote about. Sure, there were some great names there, Jack Kemp, Billy Waite, Lance Skuthorp and so on. At best, the women only got a small article about them or perhaps a few lines at the end of a long article about the men.

Besides the roughriding, there were plenty of other acts to entertain people between riding competitions. I have already mentioned my friend, Mena Val and her bicycle riding. As you know, Jewl was Mena's sister, and it was she who persuaded Mena to join Martini's, which Mena did in the middle of 1903 when we were in Cairns[92]. Until Mena joined Martini's I had not known her very well at all, but that did not last long because we soon became great mates. Of course, Jewl continued her song and dance act and was very popular with the crowds.

Then there was the time that Lance and Mart were in Sydney at the same time. The papers were giving plenty of publicity to both shows so, quite apart from the ill-feeling between to two of them, there was plenty of rivalry but, before anything else, they were great showmen. So they seized the opportunity to have a big competition between the two shows and played the publicity for all it was worth.

It took them quite a while to get everything organised but finally they settled on St Patricks Day, 17th March, 1906[93]. The place they chose for this competition was Rawson Place, Sydney.

---

[92]   This date was calculated from the itinerary of Martini's Buckjumping Show.

[93]   Jack Pollard "The Horse Tamer" Pollard Publishing Co. 1970

Why they decided to go there I will never know because the place was quite close to where the Central Railway Station now stands. At that time, the railway station was still being built so the whole area was a mess and I will tell you why.

For some reason the Old Devonshire Street Cemetery had been selected as the site for the new station and you can imagine the outcry that caused! The station could hardly be built on top of the bodies that were already buried there, so it was decided that the bodies had to be dug up and then reburied in other cemeteries, mainly Rookwood Cemetery, Waverley Cemetery and Botany Cemetery.

Many people were horrified at all this, particularly families of those people whose graves were being opened and the bodies exhumed. Distress became absolute horror when it was discovered that some of the corpses appeared to have moved in their coffins. Immediately people began to suspect that many of these corpses were not corpses when they were buried – in fact, they had been buried alive. It was too horrible to even think about. Just imagine if one was a relative of yours.

I had not met Kitty at the time of the railway station being finished, but I can remember the things she later said about all this and her fear of being buried alive[94]. She said she had never thought about that until they started moving the bodies. When that happened she was absolutely convinced that those people had been buried alive and were trying to get out of their coffins. That fear stayed with her for all the time that I knew her – maybe her whole life.

---

[94] Here I am putting words into Jessie's mouth. It was to me that Christina (Kitty) talked so much about the moving of the bodies from the Old Devonshire Street Cemetery. Her fear of being buried alive was so strong that when she died in 1952, she had requested her doctor to slash her wrist before she was buried. So vivid were the pictures she conveyed that I, too, suffer from a form of claustrophobia, particularly when it comes to going into anything underground such as a mine. DM

The railway station itself did not open until August, 1906 but, in March, people were working feverishly to get it finished as quickly as possible.[95] Still Rawson Place was just far enough away to make the contest possible.

An estimated three thousand people turned up to watch the buckjumping competition. The plan was to have Billy Waite from Martinis ride three horses provided by Lance Scuthorp and Lance himself would ride three horses provided by Mart. One of those from Martini's had to be Bobs. As it was claimed that Bobs had never been ridden for the full time, public interest was very high for a real test between man and horse.

Bobs was bred by a Mr. Sawtell from Byrimine Station near Cloncurry in Queensland. Mart had seen Bobs buck in Cloncurry and, like when he saw Dargin's Grey buck, was so impressed by the horse's performance that he bought Bobs on the spot. He saw Billy Waite ride in Proserpine about the same time and hired him, too[96].

Well, Mart was backing Bobs and Billy to win the contest for him. You should have seen the haggling that went on before the show could begin. As I recall, Mart and Lance still did not get on very well anyway, so there were a lot of disagreements to be settled. It had to be decided what sort of saddles were to be used for one thing; would they ride a set time or would they try to ride the horses to a standstill and so on. Finally, it came down to the only point which they could not agree on was just what saddle actually conformed to the type of saddle they had already agreed to use.

I think it was all showmanship, of course, but despite not liking each other very much, Lance and Mart played the negotiations for all they were worth. It definitely got the crowd going! You should have heard the moans and groans that went up when some new objection was raised and the cheers that went up when something quite trivial was agreed to.

---

95   Various reports on the opening of the new Sydney Central Railway Station.
96   Jack Pollard "The Horse Tamer" Pollard Publishing Co. 1970

At last the contest got under way. Billy rode his horses just fine but the real interest was in whether Lance could ride Bobs or Bobs would throw him as he had so many others. Bets were laid and arguments were flying but at last Bobs was ready and Lance got on his back. It was a top contest between man and horse. Bobs threw everything he had at Lance but this time Bobs was the loser – he simply could not throw Lance off his back. Boy! Did some money change hands that day! Lance had had enough riding for the night when his ride on Bobs ended and did not ride the other two horses from Mart's show. Lance had to accept that Mart had won the contest and so did not have to pay out the prize.

We stayed in Sydney for a while after that. Despite Lance riding him, Bobs still drew would-be riders who could not wait to prove how good they were. My wonderful Arnott's tin has given up this little item and I cannot resist copying it out. You should realise that this event took place after Lance had ridden Bobs. Here goes.

A

Temporary
Eclipse of a Corruscating Career.
How Clarence O'Neill Rode the Outlaw, "Bobs"

Some little time back, in Sydney, Martini, formerly famous as a triple bar performer, was running his big crowd of buckjumpers before nightly crowds of rocking, roaring, shrieking and cheering people and challenging all-comers to try and conquer, or even sit for three minutes, on his outlaw, that devil in horsehide, "Bobs".

New Zealand's champion cross-country rider, Clarence O'Neill, was one who tried. He accepted thirty pounds to ten shillings that he could not stick to Bobs for three minutes. There was much preliminary display and harangue. Clarence took off his coat and watch and chain, turned to the audience, at length, and spreading out his hands, as might a gladiator in the Roman Arena, he cried aloud, "Ladies and gentlemen, I shall do my best. You watch me ride this horse. I don't think he can throw me in a week!" And three thousand pairs of hands clapped as one as the modern St. George turned to venture a fall with the equine dragon.

They had Bobs blindfolded, his head held by a twitch and his ears, and after again testing girth and surcingle, Clarry was thrown like a feather into the saddle. He took the reins in both hands, settled himself into his seat and cried, "Let him go – watch me ri –" Like the young man of Kildare, he finished his ride in the air! Bobs wheeled on one heel, sprang 13 feet 7 inches towards the empyrean, corkscrewed up there like a dodging footballer, hit the ground with legs stiffened like iron rods and – Clarence whirled through space, rooting up the loose earth and ran like a steam plough for 14 feet 10 inches after he lit.

Dozens of the best roughriders from all parts of Australia, attracted by Martini's offer of one hundred pounds to any man who could ride Bobs, came to the centre in Sydney, but nobody took the money away.

This just goes to show what a great rider Lance was! But what the hell does corruscating mean?[97]

We moved on to Wellington. As usual, Dad turned up wanting money but got more than he bargained for! He was bunging it on as usual, bragging about his high and mighty friends and relatives – as though he had any! One bloke amongst those listening to him worked for Mart. His name was Harry Nelson but he was nicknamed "the Admiral" or "Lord Nelson".[98] Wally said he had a sister called Miss White so perhaps

---

[97] According to the Australian Concise Oxford Dictionary Third Edition, "coruscating" means 1) glitter; give flashes of light 2) show brilliance or virtuosity
[98] Wally Craven

his real name was White. Harry looked up from what he was doing and yelled out "Yah! What a joke! You with toffy mates! Don't come your fancy talk where I can hear you, Matey. We both know that we grew up in the same mean, hungry streets of London!"

Dad tried to fade into the background or make himself invisible but everyone else just roared laughing[99]. Thank heavens, Dad left me alone for a while after that.

There were plenty of acts and roughriders that would join us for a while then move on to another show. I must admit I was always glad to meet up with them again somewhere out on the road and to enjoy some good old chats about how the world was treating them.

I made friends with some blokes who worked the tents and equipment as well. I have already mentioned Wally Craven and Arthur Beale who, in later years helped me through some really bad times simply by just being there and talking about what used to be. They were kind men, too, like Mart.

Sometime during 1907 Mena sued for divorce from John Dempsey. I cannot remember what were the grounds she gave but she was really upset about it all.

It was a happy life and one that I enjoyed enormously. The constant moving from place to place never allowed one to get bored and hard work never hurt anyone because we all pitched in and helped each other. I had plenty of friends and, above all, dear Mart and Jewl were there.

And then disaster struck!

---

[99]   The story as told to Jim McJannett by Wally Craven. It is believed that the heckler was possibly a person called 'Nelson' and may have been with Jessie's father in the Royal Navy.

I will never forget Saturday, June 30, 1907! When we were in Armidale in New South Wales Mart went to get some sawdust from Nott's Sawmill with a wagonette and pair to put down in the ring for the performance that night. While the sawdust was being shovelled onto the cart, a train whistle spooked the horses. Mart fell and somehow his legs got tangled in the reins, dragging him along the ground. His legs were badly cut about so they called Doctor Harris to come and take a look. The Doc put twenty seven stitches in one leg. Mart was out cold while all this was going on, but he recovered consciousness and it seemed that he would make a full recovery. [100]

Mart seemed to be healing up just fine. Then in the evening of July 1, 1907[101] he took a sudden turn for the worse. The doctor could do nothing for him and he died during the next day, July 2, 1907[102]. He was only thirty eight. We think he must have suffered some sort of severe internal injuries that we did not know about and these were what really caused his death. It seems most unlikely that a few cuts and bruises would have been the cause.

It felt like my world collapsed around my ears on that day. Mart was just gone! I could not think past that dreadful fact. A world with no Mart was too dreadful to even think about much less understand. How much worse must it have been for Jewl.

Mart's death was reported in so many of the papers. For example, *The Sydney Morning Herald* carried notices of his death on July 3[103] and 5. Even *The Brisbane Courier*[104] reported it on July 3 and *The Weekly*

---

[100] New South Wales Death Registration 7865/1907

[101] This is also a calculated date. Martini died on July 2, 1907 but took a turn for the worse on the night before. Therefore the date of this bad turn has to be July 1, 1907.

[102] New South Wales Death Certificate 7865/1907

[103] "The Sydney Morning Herald" July 3, 1907 report of death; July 5, 1907 official death notice on page 6.

[104] "The Brisbane Courier" July 3, m 1907 report of death

Times[105] on July 6. There were probably more newspaper reports but these are the only ones I know about.

His body was taken by train to Sydney for burial in Waverley Cemetery. The funeral was held at 2.45pm on July 4, after leaving his parents' home at 121 Windsor Street, Paddington. I do not remember much about it but I know Jewl was so calm but very pale and sad. I cannot remember if she cried much but she seemed too calm for that.

The Sydney Morning Herald and *The Referee*[106] gave him lovely obituaries and from these I learned quite a bit that I did not already know about Mart. The article praised the buckjumping show and the marvellous entertainment it provided for the public. There is mention of the large number of wreaths and telegrams that were received by the family and the hundreds that followed the funeral procession to Waverley Cemetery. Reference was made to Jewel as Mart's "widow" but perhaps they were just being polite.

---

[105]   "The Weekly Times" July 6, 1907 provided additional details of accident that killed Mart.

[106]   "The Sydney Morning Herald" July 4, 1907 Funeral Section and "The Referee" July 10, 1907 Obituary

The Breheney family's headstone in Waverley Cemetery, Sydney.

Later a big headstone was built over his grave. A couple of years later his father, William, died[107]. That was in 1909, I think. Then in 1912, after the sale of the show, his mother, Julia, died and she also is buried there[108]. In later years, I would visit the grave fairly often and I can still see the inscription on the headstone as if it was in front of me now.

Martin Breheney
"J Martini, Showman"
Born Araluen 28th April, 1868
Died 2nd July, 1907
Through injuries received at Armidale"

Of course, as many of us as could be spared from caring for the animals had gone down to Sydney and became part of the hundreds who followed the coffin to Waverley[109]. I well remember the tears rolling down Billy Waite's cheeks.

Jack Prendergast was there too. Remember him? He was Mart's first star rider. Sadly, although we did not know it then, Jack was soon to follow Mart. After the funeral was over, we caught the train back to Armidale.

We sure were a miserable lot. I think I cried just about all the way there.

When we got back to Armidale, everything seemed to have changed. The joy and excitement seemed to have died with Mart. Still, the show had to go on. I must say everyone was so good. They all pulled together and helped Jewl in any way they could. For example, with Mart's death, we did not have a proper ringmaster. Jewl stepped into the job and did a really good job of it, too. The crowds believed that she was Mart's widow and I think we also got lots of sympathy from them because of that. You know the sort of thing; brave little widow fighting to keep her

---

[107]   New South Wales Death Registration 10509/1909
[108]   New South Wales Death Registration 7222/1912
[109]   "The Sydney Morning Herald" July 4, 1907

dead husband's business going. In any event, they turned up in droves; something that we were very thankful to see. She also had to attend to the actual running of the show and the strain, as well as the grief, was starting to affect her health. In fact, we were all sort of holding our breath, waiting to see what the future would bring.

Still, as they say, the show had to go on. I must say that everyone attached to the show was just so good. They all pulled together and helped Jewl in any way they could.

Billy Waite was one who really went out of his way to keep Martini's memory alive. As the months went by, the show slowly seemed to brighten up although the strain of it was still affecting Jewl.

We got one hell of a surprise about then. Not a nice surprise either. Mart had died without making a will so we just took it for granted that Jewl would inherit and we would go on as usual. Not on your life! Mart's father, William, stepped in and claimed the show although he was so old and sick and knew next to nothing about running a a buckjumping show. He said that he was Mart's next of kin and should get the show. Because Mart had not made a will, the whole show had to go for Probate and you know what happens when the legal blokes get their hands on something like this.

Added to all that, Mart's brother, Patrick, stuck his bib in and signed some legal document stating that to his certain knowledge Mart had never married[110]. Therefore, Jewl was not Mart's wife and had no claim on the Mart's estate, which was quite considerable. The Probate people found that William was the new legal owner of Martini's Buckjumping Show and valued Mart's estate at £839.7.7 (eight hundred and thirty nine pounds seven shillings and seven pence). This was broken up into livestock – £129.0.0 (one hundred and twenty nine pounds), carriages –

---

110   Statutory Declaration signed by Patrick Breheney (Mart's brother) and dated
        August 8, 1907

£25.0.0 (twenty five pounds; harness and saddles – £10.0.0 (ten pounds), other personal property – £17.0.0 (seventeen pounds) and money in the Government Savings Bank – £658.7.7 (six hundred and fifty eight pounds seven shillings and seven pence). William also asked that Patrick be appointed as his agent to manage the show. So we now had a manager that knew next to nothing about running a buckjumping show! Good thinking, wasn't it? Talk about how to send a good business broke. The probate was issued on 24th July 1907[111], so Mart's family had not wasted any time in getting in on that one.

I suppose I sound rather bitter about all that but I felt so sorry for Jewl. She had been struggling to keep things going as Mart would have liked. Now it looked like she could be kicked out! Thank heavens, it never happened.

Jewl, Harry Kennedy and Billy Waite carried on, sharing the work load between them. We all pulled together and the show toured to many places in the western part of the state. Then we headed off down the south Coast of New South Wales. As we toured, we became more and more certain that Patrick could not manage the show properly so we got more and more worried. Some of the performers left the show and who can blame them?

Then late in 1908, Jewl surprised us all by announcing she had bought William out of the show and she was now the only owner[112]. Boy, did that cheer us up! I still do not know how she managed all this but I have my suspicions.

All this uncertainty made me feel more and more miserable. I lost weight and just got more and more snappish and bad tempered.

---

[111] Probate Series 40287 or 40257. It is very difficult to read which.
[112] There is no documentation to confirm this sale but it is the only thing that satisfies later events.

CHAPTER FOUR

LIFE AFTER MART

Things were really bad following Mart's death. Everything seemed to be an effort and we were all so grumpy. I simply could not bear to watch the show slowly starting to go downhill just because we were such a miserable lot. Also it was agony watching Patrick trying to learn how to run the show. To make it worse it hurt me just to see even the smallest changes that had to be made to keep things going.

One rather sweet thing came out years later. I forget who told me about it but Mart had relatives all over the place and in quite a few states. An awful lot of them were called either William or Patrick so they must have been family names. It was only after the third son came on the scene that new names were thought about. Because we travelled to so many parts of the states we always seemed to be visiting some member of the Breheney family.

There was a cousin living in Wyalong in the central west of New South Wales. Surprise, surprise, his name was Patrick.[113] His wife was Levina.[114] They had a son in 1916 and they decided to call him James

---

[113]   Patrick Michael Breheney New South Wales Birth Certificate 2184/1862
[114]   Levina McDonald Born Jerry Berry New South Wales 1884

Martini Breheney.[115] Mart would have been so pleased about that! James was the fourth son so they were able to introduce a new name. James' two eldest brothers were named – you guessed it! – Patrick and William.[116] The next brother was John.[117]

To me the show was my last link with Mart – to a part of my life that was gone forever. I had to force myself to do anything but my heart was not in it. I grieved for Mart; for the kindness that I might never find again; for the security and protection that he had given me. It just seemed that the light had gone out of my life.

I was such a wet blanket that Jewl suggested that I take a holiday away from the show. At first I refused but the more I thought about it the more it seemed like it was not such a bad idea. New Zealand! I would just love to see that country. I had heard so much about it and perhaps the change of scenery would do me good. I had some money of my own and Jewl offered to help with the expenses so I decided to go.

I should have known better. My bad luck followed me across the Tasman. The trip started well enough. I was not seasick for a start which was promising. When I reached New Zealand, I discovered why everyone was so fascinated with the scenery. It was magic. The two things that stand out in my mind even after all these years were the hot springs and mud baths at Rotorua, and the Blue and Green Lakes.[118] I had never seen anything like the mud pools. It was just like a big pot of soup or stew simmering away on a stove. Only this was happening in the ground.

---

[115] Born at Wyalong, New South Wales, December 14, 1916.

[116] Patrick William Born Victoria 1905. William New South Wales Birth Registration 6230/1909

[117] John born 1914. Information obtained from local records

[118] My grandmother, Christina (Kitty) often mentioned Rotorua and the Blue and Green Lakes to me when I was a child. Obviously they made a great impression on her so I have included them here although there is no certainty that Jess ever visited them.DM

The Blue and Green Lakes were another sight that I will never forget. On one side of this narrow strip of land was the Blue Lake. As its name suggests, it was this most beautiful clear blue but on the other side of the strip was this brilliant clear green lake. Now, how could that be? Why were they two different colours? What could have been the reason? Oh, it was a beautiful, beautiful land!

But the ache of missing Mart never really went away. It was with me wherever I went. I tried to make friends with people but I think I just frightened them off – or perhaps just repelled them with the way I talked. I certainly did not have a la-de-dah accent which seemed to upset some people. This was made worse because I often felt just plain cranky or irritable which in turn made me very quick to bite someone's head off. I certainly was not good company for those who were out to enjoy a pleasant holiday!

When I got to Wanganui, I found there was a circus playing there. Yes, it drew me like a magnet! Foolish, you say? Well, of course it was foolish to go and stir up all those memories when I should have been trying to put them in the past. But that did not stop me from going to the circus. I paid my money and went up into the seating stands. Just sitting there looking around me made me feel like I had come home. And of course all those memories came tumbling into my mind – memories that I was trying so hard to bury. I was just sitting there, looking around and enjoying the smells and the noises, lost in those memories, when there was an almighty crack and the stand where I was collapsed. Down I went with all that breaking timber and stuff.

The local newspaper gave a report of this accident,[119] saying that eleven people were injured that day and I was one of them. Just my luck. They told me I had been unconscious for quite a while after they pulled me out of the wreckage. When I finally came to, they were

---

[119] The Wanganui Herald and The Evening Post April 21, 1908

still trying to get people out from under the mess of broken timber. I had a dreadful headache but insisted I was alright – all I wanted to do was to go back to the boarding house where I was staying and just lie down.

This all happened in April, 1908 – I seem to remember it was the 20[th][120] –but it was to cast a shadow over the rest of my life. Those headaches that I started to get after that accident have continued over the years, gradually getting worse. I suspect that this accident may have had something to do with these headaches and the thing I have in my head now.

---

[120]   The Wanganui Herald and The Evening Post April 21, 1908

A young Christina Margaret Bellati. She is wearing a lovely
dress she is believed to have made herself.

When I was feeling a bit better, I decided to continue with my holiday. It was then that I met Kitty and Paul Bellati[121] who were staying at the same hotel that I went to. It was a really posh place and I should have known better than to stay there. Talk about a fish out of water! Kitty and Paul who were on their honeymoon[122] were already staying there when I arrived. They did not seem to mind the way I talked. After all, Paul, who I later learnt was an Italian, had a pretty strong accent so maybe they did not notice mine.

They seemed quite happy to talk to me and we sometimes sat together when we had our evening meal. They were not stuck up like the other guests. I liked Kitty very much and Paul was quite nice too. Kitty was about my age, eighteen, but Paul was a lot older.

Our friendship started when I came into the main dining room one evening soon after I arrived at the hotel. The dining room really made me nervous. I knew my table manners were not the best and some of the other guests had been rather snooty about our meals. There was a very fancy dining room there with a rather long dining table in it. It so happened that I sat down on the left of Kitty while Paul was on her right. I had already been talking to Kitty during the afternoon so it seemed just natural to sit with them.

It was obvious that Kitty came from a well-off family but she was awfully kind to me, kinder than anyone else in that place. She did not seem to mind how rough I talked – not like the other guests. Kitty told me that Paul had been born in Turin in Italy. He was nice too but any fool could see that he only had eyes for Kitty.

---

[121] It is not known if the Bellatis and Jess met in New Zealand but the dates of the accident and of the Bellatis marriage are suggestive. This is also supported by some photos of the Bellati's trip.

[122] The Bellatis married April 28, 1908. This coupled with Kitty's repeated mentions of her trip to New Zealand suggests that is where they honeymooned and it is entirely possible that they met Jess there.DM

And no wonder! Kitty was beautiful. Very tall with lovely chestnutty hair, beautiful skin and boy, could she dress well! She talked like a lady too. In fact, she looked like a lady from head to toe. Add to all this, she was lively, had a great sense of humour and seemed to get on well with anyone and everyone. No wonder I liked her so much.

Well, this had been a busy day for me so I was rather hot, tired and thirsty when I went in for the evening meal. When I saw glasses of water out on the table I grabbed one exclaiming "Oh, good!! I am so thirsty!" and tossed it off.[123] There was dead silence so I knew I had done something wrong. Then Kitty commented on the weather and what a beautiful day it had been and everyone started talking again. She later explained to me that the glass of water was a finger bowl to be used only for rinsing your fingers after eating something a bit messy - like those fish things we had for tea that night. You did not lick your fingers afterwards like I always did, oh, dear me, no! How the hell was I to know that you were supposed to wash your fingers in the damned bowl???

Who was to know that the simple act of drinking the water in a finger bowl would play such an important part on our future lives. But that comes later.

Kitty and I became quite good friends during the next few days. I know some of the other guests looked down on us both but that did not seem to bother Kitty - I think it bothered me more than it did her.

We talked together quite a bit and even went shopping occasionally. Kitty was absolutely fascinated with me being a roughrider with Martini's. She loved going to circuses and buckjumping shows and could not believe it when I told her I worked in one of those. Perhaps that is why she would help me when I made some awful blues and offended some of

---

123   This is another story that Kitty told me and fits in very well with what is known of Jess. Kitty did not name Jess but, at the time, she was using this event to impress on me how bad table manners could be very embarrassing. DM

the other guests. With Kitty's help, I was really trying to do the right thing but most of them were really snooty and I was sorry I had not chosen somewhere else to stay. But then I might never have met Kitty. So perhaps I did have some good luck there.

It seems her Dad was often at sea so when she decided to marry Paul it meant she had to get William's consent to the marriage. This was because she was only eighteen and could not marry until she was twenty one without her parent's consent. How could she get that when she did not know where he was? Simple! They went to a Court and got permission from there. I was to discover later that when Kitty made up her mind about something she usually got it. Gosh, we never seemed to stop talking. What with her interest in travelling shows and my interest in her and her way of life, who can wonder at that?

I learned quite a bit about Kitty, too. Her father was William Alexander Nicol.[124] He was the Superintending Engineer with the Port Jackson Steamship Co. Her mother had died in 1892 when Kitty was only two, leaving her and her sister, Jean[125].

With two young daughters to care for, her Dad was not long in remarrying. He was often as sea which must have made caring for the girls a big problem. He married Hilda Smith the following year which solved that problem for him. He and Hilda had four children over the following years.[126]

---

[124] Born Glasgow, Scotland June 21, 1858 Married Margaret Love (Kitty's Mother) in Brisbane, Queensland, September 9, 1884

[125] Jane, known as Jean, born Kiama New South Wales Birth Registration 25095/1886; married John Henry Rayner New South Wales Marriage Registration 6702/1907 New South Wales Death Registration 2447/1958

[126] Hilda Smith New South Wales Marriage Registration 6702/1893; William New South Wales Birth Registration 16277/1897; Hilda New South Wales Birth Registration 3721/1904; Glennifie New South Wales Birth Registration 18001/1906 and Herbert in 1908.

To my regret it was not long before Kitty and Paul had to move on to the next place they were to visit so Kitty and I had to say goodbye. Kitty gave me her address in Australia making me promise to at least write to her there. I told her that a letter addressed to me at Martini's Buckjumping Show would probably catch up with me eventually. In any event, I could always visit her when we were in Sydney. And so we parted. I had not been feeling so good after the accident at Wanganui so I decided to go home. I spent a few more days just looking around before booking a passage back to Australia.

Sometime towards the end of 1908 Jewl had managed to buy William out of the show and become the sole proprietor. It was a big job and I do not know where she found the money to do this but she did. It was a good job she did because Martinis was starting to struggle and needed a good manager running it.[127]

Mart had been a terrific promoter of the show and Jewl showed she had a great talent there, too. The show had continued to operate and during the months after Mart's death and into 1908 we appeared at Gunnedah, Werris Creek, Murrurundi, Singleton, Maitland, Newcastle, Wallsend and Parramatta. After a short spell we then headed down the south coast of New South Wales.[128] After all, a travelling show must do that – travel, I mean – but Jewl made sure that people knew well ahead when we were coming to town. At first there was a lot of sympathy for Jewl because the crowds just flocked to see what we had to offer now Mart was gone.

When the proprietors of other shows realised that Jewl did not have the support of either William or Patrick Breheney, they started to make life difficult for Jewl in an effort to force her to sell. None of us at Martini's needed that – particularly Jewl! They maintained it was no job for a woman and she should sell up and enjoy the money she got for the show.

---

[127] It is possible that Mick Ryan provided the money but this is not certain.
[128] This itinerary has been compiled from newspaper advertisements etc. for this period.

Try telling that to Mary Ann Gould who kept Jack Daly's show running while he did three years in Pentridge!

Good old *Stageland* and *Referee* supported us by giving us plenty of editorials and advertising generally about what we were doing and keeping Martini's in the public eye.

Mart was supposed to have copyrighted the title of "Fun in a Stockyard"[129] and some of these bludgers started the same act but changed the name to "Fun in THE Stockyard". They claimed they were not infringing copyright then. Well, I do not know about that but it seemed to me to be a pretty low thing to do.

Another lying rumour was started saying that Bobs had been sold and a ring-in was being shown at Martini's. This was, of course, untrue. Jewl soon dealt with that by publishing a detailed description of Bobs again and warning the public not to be taken in by some look-alike of Bobs. I could not help wondering how many people would believe that it was not Bobs at Martini's and continue to believe it in the face of the fact that one only had to see Bobs buck to know that he was not a ring-in! People would not pay good money to see a champion if they thought they might be fobbed off with a ring-in. Talk about sneaks and dirty tricks.

I like that bit that *Stageland* put in one of their editorials about Martini's. *Stageland* certainly got stuck into them in an editorial headed *Dingoes Dog a Lonely Ewe*[130]. They said that Jewl was trying to keep the show going "in spite of the dastardly and continued efforts of a set of cowardly woman-baiters to injure her." That's telling 'em!

Jewl was quite capable of running Martini's if these miserable sods had left her alone, but with them snapping at her heels all the time she had

---

[129] "Fun in a Stockyard" The Referee, September 10, 1906
[130] Stageland February 26, 1908

to do something. Most of this had started while I was in New Zealand and was a nasty surprise when I got back to Martini's.

When I did get back to the show, I could see that Jewl was really struggling to keep things under control. Protecting the animals, dealing with rowdy crowds as well the day to day running of things must have been hell for her! Jewl said she was as glad to have me back as I was to be back. That made me feel better and I plunged into giving her all the help I could so the work soon took over my life again as the show had to go on as the saying goes.

Jewl was right, the holiday in New Zealand had done me good. Except for the crack on my head of course.

We had to keep our eye on these louts but the show was popular still, so we were able to keep our heads above water.

By the end of 1908 I was starting to get on with my life again. It had taken a long time for me to accept Mart's death and be interested in what was going on around me. Then as a sad start to the new year, 1909 that is, dear old Dargin's Grey died near Nyngan in New South Wales on January 11, 1909. He was old – twenty nine to be exact but it still came as a blow.[131] Mart had loved this horse so much and admired his fighting spirit. I felt that another link to Mart had gone. Soon I would be left with only my memories.

During our travels, Jewl had met up with Mick Ryan, who was described as a "Brisbane sportsman". I knew they became very friendly and liked to meet up when they were both in Brisbane. Even so, it came as quite a shock when I learnt that they had married in Dubbo on January 27, 1909.[132] How could she do such a thing? It took me a while to come to

---

131 The Referee January20, 1909
132 The Referee February 17, 1909

see that it may only have been a marriage of convenience to keep the show going or make things easier for Jewl. At least that is what I told myself. She just couldn't have forgotten Mart in only eighteen months!

The best thing was that it certainly put a stop to all that bullying. Those wretches soon pulled their heads in when they found she had married Mick. Still, it made me sad to see her with someone other than Mart. We all knew that Jewl could run a show as well as any man – and did – but those mongrels just had to pick on her because "women can't run shows like that". How I hate this contempt those sort of people have for the abilities of women! Well, they lost this fight – Martini's stayed with Jewl.

What a month! First the Grey dying and then Jewl getting married – not that I am saying they are the same sort of thing but neither could be expected to cheer me up.

Then just to cap it all off, Jewl took sick.[133] We did not know what was wrong with her but my guess is that it was the relief of getting those bullies and their dreadful behaviour off her back. Anyway, by April she was much better and hotly denying that Martini's was connected with any other show in Australia.[134] Just to prove she was back, she was challenging any rider in Australia to ride either Bobs or Trouble under her conditions.

The following months were hard for me. My health was not really good although it was slowly getting better. The constant hard work of touring through New South Wales, Victoria and Queensland was not much help either. Funny how things come back to you. I remember once when we were in Nowra, Jewl complained bitterly that it cost 6d[135] for a bale of hay. She had to cough it up because our animals had

133 The Referee April 11, 1909
134 The Referee April 11, 1909
135 Six pence. Fifty cents in Australian decimal currency.

to be fed if they were to perform well. Usually, when we were on the coastal roads we relied on green pick in the long paddock[136] to lower the costs of feeding the animals. I wonder why I should remember that now? I expect it is just one of those little niggling things that stick in your mind.

During those years, I would make time to catch up with Kitty whenever we were in Sydney. Her marriage was not going well and she was terribly unhappy. Sometimes she would visit me at the show but most times I went to her. Looking back, we must have been a pretty miserable pair but somehow that seemed to strengthen our friendship.

One day, a young bloke came up to where Jewl and I were looking at a new horse. He wanted a job as a rigger. Jewl looked him up and down and asked, "Any experience?"

The young bloke threw back his head and laughed. "Lady," he said, "I am in the Royal Navy and can outrig any rigger you have here!"

Jewl laughed too. "Hmmmm! Modest too, I see! OK, if you are in the Royal Navy, how long will you be here before you sail again? We do not expect to be here long ourselves so you might find yourself without a job before your ship sails."

"Don't worry" said the young bloke. "I am only after some more cash. I am afraid I spent up rather well this leave so anything will help. Just tell me what you want done."

---

[136]   Slang for "green grass along the roadside"

Jewl took him on. He said his name was Ben Hickman[137] and he was with the *HMS Terrible*.[138] He was right – he was a good rigger. From then on, if we were both in town at the same time, he had a job with Martini's. It was all pretty casual but we all liked him and saw quite of a bit of him from then on.

---

[137] This scene comes purely from my imagination. Ben Hickman did work with Martini's from time to time, whenever his ship was in port but something along the lines of this scene would probably have taken place when he first applied for a casual job as rigger.

[138] Royal Navy Records 198730

Benjamin Walter Hickman. Ben was regarded as a well dressed man. This is evidenced by the jaunty angle of his hat, the flower in his lapel and his impeccable suit.

In 1910 he had been transferred to the *HMS Powerful* and promoted to a Leading Seaman. He was so proud of himself and I was pleased for him, too, because he was a nice bloke.[139]

Mick and Jewl worked very hard but I think it was all getting too much for them. Mick had commitments other than Martini's, but I think that the real problem was that Mick did not have Mart's passion for the travelling show. This could have rubbed off on Jewl because she seemed to be losing heart as well. Her getting sick now and again had made things worse. In fact, we could all see that the show was in trouble. It was hard to know what to do or how to tackle the problem.

Added to everything else, Billy Waite who had been such a help when Mart died back in 1907, decided to join with Lytton's. Like Mart, he really had wanted his own show but did not have the heart to leave while Mart was there. They were really good mates.

The show gave its last performance in February, 1910 and that almost broke my heart. I simply fled to Kitty for comfort.

I flung myself into her arms sobbing miserably. "Oh, Kitty," I wailed, "they have closed Martini's down. Jewl and Mick are looking for a buyer!"

Dear, practical Kitty just patted me gently on the shoulder and said, "Come inside and I'll make us both a nice cup of tea and you can tell me all about it." I trailed into the kitchen, no doubt looking just as sad as I felt. Kitty put the kettle on, got the cups, milk and so on and then made tea.

---

[139] In a discussion with Jim McJannett, Wally Craven gave the following description "Ben Hickman was a bit of a mystery. It was obvious he had a naval background because it was his skills as a rigger that brought him into contact with the circus. He was hired from time to time for rigging work."

The whole story poured out of me as we sipped the very hot tea and nibbled the biscuits that were still warm from the oven. Kitty was thoughtful for a while.

"What are you going to do now?" she asked.

"How the hell do I know?" I snapped.

"Well, you can think as clearly as possible and try to figure out a plan," she replied. She suggested a few things but I was not having any of them. No horses. Eventually, I went home, nearly as miserable as when I arrived.

The show was advertised for sale in the *Referee*[140] but little interest was shown by other buckjumping shows.

It must have seemed like a gift from the gods when Michael Augustine Ferry[141] (a well known horse-breeder, dealer and shipper of horses as well as an ABC commentator) and Alf Neave[142] (Dorham Doolette's right hand man of business and managing director of Wild Australia) came with an offer to buy the show on behalf of Dorham Doolette, well known as the owner of the Bullfinch Gold Mine in Western Australia.[143] Alf Neave was an English-born West Australian cattleman who had married a sister of Dorham Doolette.

Doolette planned to combine Martini's with Philip Lytton's Australian Roughriders to form one big group and take them to England under the name of *Wild Australia*. It was a twofold plan. One part was to promote the Bullfinch Mine in England and the other was to take part in the coronation celebrations of George V in July, 1911.

---

[140] Wednesday, 4th May, 1910 issue
[141] Thorpe McConville's Wild Australia
[142] Thorpe McConville's Wild Australia
[143] Jenny Hicks "Australian Cowboys, Roughriders and Rodeos" Harper & Collins Publishers Pty Ltd

The offer was too good to refuse, particularly as Doolette meant to take most of the performers and animals from both Martini's and Lytton's to England. Most of the Martini's people took up the offer to go to England, sailing on the SS *Sussex* which left here on March 14, 1911. Some very good roughriders went to England - roughriders like Billy Waite from Cloncurry, Jack Morrissey, Hawkins from Queensland, Thorpe McConville, Billy Jonas, Billy Lee, Ned Lloyd (he was a nephew of Ned Kelly) and Pascoe from New Zealand.[144] They were all top notch riders and what a show they could put on!

I remember that Cleo and Bonita[145] were amongst the performers who sailed on the *Sussex*. Bobs was part of the deal too and he and another famous buckjumper called Snips were sold to Doolette. Neither returned to Australia, either dying either on the way to England or in England.[146]

When the news of the sale was broken to me, I knew that part of my life was over. Only memories of Mart, Jewl and the others, both human and animal remained. The rest was gone forever.

I did screw up the courage to go down to the ship when they all sailed for England. After all, it was quite an honour to be taking such an important part in the coronation celebrations so how could I be such a wet blanket and throw doom and gloom on their great adventure? How could I spoil all that? I waved them off quite cheerily until I could no longer make them out at the rail then turned sadly to face what I saw then as a very bleak future.

---

[144] "Who's Who in Wild Australia" and "The Morning Advertiser" London May 22, 1911

[145] "Who's Who in Wild Australia" and "The Pageant of Empire – Wild Australia"

[146] The fate of Snips is recorded in "Thorpe McConville's Wild Australia". Poor Snips never made it to England. Tex Morton, well-known entertainer of yesteryear, told Jim McJannett in 1967 that, while in England, Bobs broke his leg while being loaded onto a float and had to be destroyed. Despite a diligent search, Jim has been unable to find any documentation to support this story. But if true, what a sad end for such a great horse!

What happened when they got to England? As was only to be expected, the show created quite a stir there. Crowds flocked to see them and it played a prominent part in the celebrations in London. I did hear that the King and Queen were so impressed with the show that they went a second time to enjoy the exciting atmosphere.[147]

After the coronation, Alf Neave took *Wild Australia*, as it was known then, on tour in some of the counties, finally selling the whole show to a well-known British showman, Francis C Bostock, known as "Little Frank".[148] When that cold British winter struck, the show collapsed and some of the performers came back to Australia while others decided to try their luck in America.

Thorpe McConville had a lucky escape, though. He was booked to sail on the *Titanic* but he needed to get to America in a hurry so he changed his booking to the *Lusitania* which sailed before the *Titanic*[149]. Was his guardian angel looking after him or what?

You can see that I kept in touch with some of my old friends from Martini's and they sent me scraps of news about some of the others. Also, I met up with Wally and Arthur from time to time and we swapped news then but I really did miss the travel and excitement of the show.

---

[147]   Thorpe McConville's Wild Australia
[148]   Thorpe McConville's Wild Australia
[149]   Thorpe McConville's Wild Australia

CHAPTER FIVE

TRIALS AND TRIBULATIONS

After the sale of the show was settled, we all went our separate ways as you can imagine. I must admit that Jewl and Mick paid us all off and even gave us a generous bonus.[150]

Somehow, I could not have faced joining another show. I do not know why I felt that way but I had enjoyed such a favoured position with Martini's that I was sure I could never go back to those happy 'before Mart' days. Besides, since the accident in New Zealand, my health was not as good as it should be. I was still getting those dreadful headaches. Perhaps they would ease if I chose a less energetic way of life.

Nor did I want to get married. I was pretty sure Ben would have jumped at the chance but I liked being independent and not a sort of unpaid servant. No, marriage was out. What I really wanted was to be able to please myself what I did, when I did it and where I did it.

---

[150] This and the following account of Jessie's movements following the breakup of Martini's Buckjumpers is as told by Wally Craven.

While I was still deciding what to do with myself, I had a good time spending the money that Jewl had given me. And, boy, did I have a good time!

I met up with a young bloke by the name of Carmody and a mate of his called Mick Fox. We decided we would go up the the Gulf Country of Queensland to muster cattle, drove and do some horsebreaking. After all, there was plenty of work there for good horsemen and I knew I met that standard.

In the end, they went without me because I was too busy spending money in Sydney. I started breaking in ponies when the money started to run low but I sort of just drifted from job to job and place to place. At one time, I had digs at The Rocks in Sydney.

You could say that I just drifted along not really knowing or caring what happened next. You know, I really think that I just could not get over the sale of Martini's.

Thanks to Mum, I could read and write, which was more than a lot of people could do, but I was still not good enough at these to use them to support myself. Besides, it would mean working indoors and after my roving life with Martini's I was not sure I could handle that.

Maybe I could be some sort of servant but I did not like being ordered around by anyone so that did not seem a good idea. I could do the hard work – that was nothing – but I knew I would feel like a slave! I knew then that I would have to get work around horses.

I could certainly ride really well and I knew how to move cattle around so perhaps I should find something there. I used the last of what little money I had left to start a riding school at O'Meara Street in Kogarah. One advantage was that the school was near Wally's brother's place so I got to see quite a bit of Wally as well as his brother.

It was only a small riding school on rented land but I did try to make a go of it. It never did really succeed so I started to steal things to keep myself and the horses fed. At first it was only food but then I would take anything I could sell to get money for the rent. That had to be paid if I was to keep the school going.

Sometimes I would take one of Jean Rayner's girls up in front of me when I took the horses down to Kogarah Bay for a swim. They were good kids and loved a ride on the horses or just watching them having their swim.

I still had to have somewhere to live so I moved in with my McIntyre relatives at Bankstown. They worked a small property there and were prepared to let me stay with them for a while. It also seemed a good idea to change my name, too, so I became Jessie McIntyre for the next eight or nine years. That kept things simple with no explanations needed for nosey neighbours.

Then quite unexpectedly, Ben Hickman popped in one day for a visit. We had a great time and when he had to go back to his ship he gave me some money to help keep myself going with the riding school. He was very sweet about it all. It was quite obvious that he liked me so it came as no surprise that he would drop in to see me whenever his ship was in Sydney. We would have a good time together and when he was leaving he would give me some money.

I liked Ben. He was fun to be with and I always felt better after a visit from him. Life was not so bad then, but I was still lonely in spite of the brood of McIntyres. How I missed Mart, Jewl and the circus life! Occasionally, Wally would drop in for a cuppa and we would talk about Mart and his show and other memories we had. That helped me, too, but I was determined I would live my life the way I wanted from now on. I dreamed of having a small property somewhere in the country where I could run my horses and make a living for myself. In the meantime I was content with what I had.

The big shock came when Ben dropped in one day, around June, 1911, I think it was, to tell me that he was leaving the navy and settling in

Australia! I was surprised that he would give up what was a promising career in the navy, but he explained that he wanted to be near me. We could talk about that later, he said. Here was another decision. He was very understanding about me not wanting to get married, but I could not see why we couldn't we just keep going the way we were?

Ben did not ask me to marry him, but as time went by it became more and more obvious that he was looking for a more settled domestic arrangement. What was I to do? I knew if I stayed with Ben, he would see that I was safe and cared for but he would expect us to live in Sydney. I would have to settle down to being an ordinary housewife – perhaps even marry him in due course, maybe even have a family. It was a big decision for me to make, but I finally decided that a safe, protected life was not for me. Give me the excitement of the road any time! Or maybe a small property of my own in the bush.

Before Ben left the Royal Navy he had been steadily working his way up through the ranks. In other words, he seemed to be a steady and reliable man. I think that is what persuaded me to give it a try. Perhaps I could be happy with him, after all. I decided I would just move in with him and see how it all went. If I was happy with the arrangement then I would think about something permanent - like marriage.

Ben must have accepted this at the beginning. Perhaps he was hoping to be able to persuade me after we lived together for a while.

Then fate decided to deal me another blow. In August, 1912 I discovered I was pregnant! It was just too much for me to cope with. A baby! Devoting my days to looking after a baby who would take so much of my day and then Ben would be home to take what was left. What about my horses? What about my freedom to choose my own life? Maybe I should give the baby away. But who would take it? Why could things not be as simple as they were in the circus? There you just did whatever had to be done and got on with life.

There were those crossroads again and I had to make a decision about what I would do. One thing, I intended to have the baby because I had heard too many dreadful stories about girls who had tried to get rid of a baby and finished up crippled or even dead. No thank you!

So what was I to do? The first thing was to finally make a decision about whether I should marry Ben and settle down as a wife and mother. I am sure Ben would have wanted that but did I? No, I did not. Me, tied to a house, dirty washing, a screaming baby? I knew I was not made for that life. Again, no thank you!

I could, I suppose, keep the baby with me or possibly pay someone else to look after him. (I did not know then if the baby would be a boy or a girl but, as I now know I had a son, I will refer to 'him'). The type of life I was thinking about did not include a child of any age. How was I to pay someone to look after him? I could not rely on Ben doing so, although it was just possible I might persuade him to. Besides there were some pretty awful stories about baby farming (as it was called) with the babies being murdered and the money kept. I could not do that to my baby, either.

So what was left? Then it hit me. Kitty! If she would agree to my idea, she was the answer to my problem. I might even be the answer to hers.

Remember I said that Kitty and I had kept in touch? Poor Kitty had been having a pretty rough time of it too. She and Paul were happy enough when I met them in New Zealand but things went wrong pretty soon after that. Perhaps it was the age difference or maybe the difference in their nationalities. I think religion came into it a bit too. She hardly ever spoke of it but she was so very sad that she did not have a baby of her own. Perhaps she and Paul could have been happy if there had been a baby, but it did not work out that way. Dear Kitty. She was such a good listener who was always ready to offer sympathy to anyone and here she was in such need of it herself. It was a shame to see her so unhappy.

Even so, it was to her I fled to pour out all my woes. She had met Ben too on various occasions when Ben was in Sydney on leave. By the time I am talking about now, she and Paul had definitely separated – somewhere around 1911 I think – and she was very lonely.

She had gone against family wishes when she got Court permission to marry Paul so she was not very popular with them. Being very independent, she had decided to support herself with dressmaking. I daresay her father may have helped her, but she still insisted on going her own way. She did not do too badly either as she was really very good at sewing. She did make some lovely things, including most of her own clothes so she was always smartly dressed. She said that was the best way to let people see what you could do – a sort of cheap way of advertising your skills, I expect.

Like Ben, Kitty was horrified that I wanted to give my baby to her to raise. At first she blamed Ben, but then she realised that it was me who did not want the baby, not Ben. We talked for hours trying to sort it all out. Finally, much against her will, she agreed to take the baby and raise it as her own child. She was sure she would be able to support herself and the child with her sewing, so that seemed the best solution for everyone. Kitty would have the baby she was so desperate to have and I would be free to do as I liked.

We agreed that I was to give birth to the baby at one of my relatives' place. Kitty would get the baby as soon as possible after he was born. She suggested that she should register the birth showing Paul as the father and herself the mother. I thought that was very clever of her because it would make it very difficult for anyone to prove that the baby was not hers. I had thought that the McIntyres might take him, but Kitty would probably be able to do more for him when he got older than the McIntyres would. I thought I had been quite clever too. I had provided for my baby's future (although I did not want him myself, I did not wish him any harm), given Kitty the baby she so wanted and set myself up for a life of freedom.

Well, I suppose it will come as no surprise that Ben was absolutely furious when I told him what we had planned. He really went to town on me! He wanted his child to be brought up in a proper home; what sort of a woman was I to give my baby away even to a friend; he wanted to be with his child. All that sort of thing. I could not get him to understand that the domesticity he wanted was simply not for me; that what I planned was best for everyone. He was so stubborn about it all!

I will never understand why Kitty was so keen to have a baby but she was and this seemed to me to be the perfect way to solve a lot of problems. I only asked one thing of Kitty. That was that the child be called Hedley if it was a boy. Rupert was added to that. I suspect that was because Ben had served on a ship called *Rupert* way back in 1901.

Ben had stormed off threatening to have nothing more to do with me. Well, that was just fine with me! He knew that Kitty was very keen on him and even threatened to move in with her so that he could be with his child. That was fine with me, too! I have to say this for Ben though – he looked after me until the baby was born. This meant that I was able to have quite a healthy pregnancy because I did not have to starve or do heavy work as so many other women had to. That does not mean I enjoyed the pregnancy though. I would just as soon be kicked by a horse!

Strangely enough, I was rather excited at first about being pregnant but that soon wore off! Tied to a house when all I wanted to do was to get on a horse and go for a gallop. Then finally Hedley Rupert was born on March 6, 1913, a birth with all the pain and trouble that a birth involves. They told me it was a perfectly normal birth and nothing to worry about. Yeah! All that for an unsightly scrap of a human being that cried, made a mess and demanded so much attention – attention I was not interested in giving. Even worse, I still had to stay in bed until I recovered my strength!

As planned, Kitty registered the birth, giving Paul and herself as the parents, on March 18, 1913 at the District Registrar at Waverley. She was smart enough not to give the Bankstown address as the place of birth. What she gave was 19 Mead Street, Waverley. I never thought of that!

Kitty was rapt with the baby right from the very start. Well, she could have him! You should have seen the love in her face when she finally held Hedley in her arms! It was then that I was absolutely sure that I had done the right thing for my son. Kitty would wrap him in love for the rest of her life and be the mother I never could be.

I knew I would be criticised for giving my son away, but I knew he would be miserable if I kept him because I would be such a terrible mother and housewife.

When Ben realised that I had really given the baby to Kitty, he made good his threat to move in with Kitty and Hedley. I forgot to mention that when Kitty registered Hedley's birth, she gave his name as Hedley Rupert Hickman Bellati. I suppose she felt that Hedley's real Dad should get a mention but Paul never recognised Hedley as his child and who can blame him for that?

When Kitty and Ben moved in together she dropped Kitty as her name, changing it to Glen. Everyone, except me, called her that from then on. She had a younger sister called Gleniffie which made me wonder if there was some connection there. As Ben and Kitty were living together as man and wife, they were called Mr and Mrs Hickman. Effectively, Kitty Bellati had become Glen Hickman.

Kitty's father, William Nicol, died in May, 1914 when Hedley was only about fourteen months old. After that Kitty rarely mentioned her father or stepmother and half brothers and sisters except to mention Billy occasionally. He was the closest to her in age and they probably were playmates during their childhood. I wondered if there was some family ill feeling about her leaving Paul, taking Hedley and moving in with Ben. They were very strict Presbyterians, you know.

I saw Glen, as she was now known, from time to time but I tried to avoid meeting Ben. It could only make trouble and I was only too happy to have Glen raise the baby to make things difficult for her. Surprisingly, I found that I was grateful that Kitty did not object to me seeing Hedley occasionally. So I was able to get to know him a bit. He was a good looking lad I must admit. Kitty also trained him well, making him awfully polite and well mannered. Trust Kitty!

Things got a bit difficult when Hedley got a bit older and started asking awkward questions. Such as who I was and where did I live? Did I know Daddy? That sort of thing. He was as sharp as a tack and always wanting to know the where and why of everything.

From then on I would only visit Kitty and Hedley when Ben was at work. Ben had got a job as a cleaner at Prouds Ltd. So they had become quite the little family with a routine so I could tell when to visit Kitty when she was alone. Even so I did not regret giving Hedley to Kitty.

I still visited Jean, Kitty's sister, whenever I wanted to and she would fill me in on what was going on in the Hickman household. Even now I get letters from her telling me about Hedley and how he is going. That is how I know that I am now a grandmother. Dear me, that seems so very, very strange to me! Jean has been a really good friend to me. Over the years her letters have convinced me that I did the right thing when I gave Hedley to Kitty, because I can see that everything I hoped for was working out well.

As for me, things were difficult even though I only had myself to provide for. I was still living with my McIntyre relations at Bankstown so I had somewhere to stay. As they had enough trouble feeding themselves let alone me, I took to stealing to sort of pay my way with them and to provide extra food and clothing for them as well.

It was not hard to do because I had learnt to steal while I was in the circus, but there I had the backup of people who would lie for me to give me some sort alibi. Of course, I repaid the favour when they struck a spot of trouble. Now I felt I could not get my relatives into trouble by asking them to lie for me.

In June and July of 1913, I was busy 'finding' things. Unfortunately, the law soon got to hear of this and came looking for me. Eventually, they caught up with me. Sadly, I could not lie my way out of this. I was charged with stealing a horse, three horse rugs, thirteen fowls, four ducks and of receiving. These were the things that they knew about, but I promise you there was plenty more they did not know about.

Mr F W Todhunter appeared for me when I went to court. You should have heard the sob story he pitched! He claimed I was married but, as my husband belonged to a well known and respectable family, I had refused to give my married name. I was supposed to have lost my parents at an early age and then lived with a circus. Well, that was true enough. Mr Todhunter went on to say that I had led a roving life as a rider with Martini's circus; was now living a lonely life at Bankstown and had fallen a victim to temptation. Wasn't that a pathetic tale?

This photo of Jessie was taken in Darlinghurst Gaol before
going to Long Bay Reformatory to serve out her sentence.
Photo courtesy of John Partridge,
formerly of the Corrective Services

I was found guilty, of course, and had to wait anxiously for sentencing. Judge Scholes who presided over the court seemed a nice old bloke. He had listened carefully to what the witnesses and Mr Todhunter said and was quite sympathetic. He considered my present position was the result of poor environment so it would be kinder to send me to Long Bay Reformatory than to give me a prison sentence. Remember I was twenty two by then and could have got a full adult sentence. Judge Scholes hoped the reformatory would teach me better ways when he sentenced me to twelve months at Long Bay.

It was not much use making trouble in the reformatory as that could lead to my sentence being extended. That was no good to me. I wanted out of there as soon as possible. With all this in mind, I decided to cop it sweet, behave myself and do what I was told.

My good behaviour resulted in an early release on licence. That did not mean I was free to go where I liked, but at least I was out of prison. I was sent for some months to some family whose name I forget until my sentence expired on August 15, 1914. It felt just great to be able to do what I liked again.

I did not think it was a good idea to go back to the McIntyres again so I looked around until I found a small place at the Oaks. While I was there I met Phillip James. It was not long before we started making ends meet by doing a little stealing. We got more and more daring until the law caught up with us. We were charged with stealing a saddle; breeching; reins; articles of clothing and household linen.

Judge Rogers was the judge this time and he was not as sympathetic as good old Judge Scholes. Judge Rogers had the nerve to say that I led Phil astray! The nerve of him! Phil did not need any leading – we were both as guilty as each other! Despite pleas for clemency Phil got fifteen months hard labour at Goulburn Gaol and I got one year and nine months at Long Bay Penitentiary. No Reformatory for me this time!

Female prisoners exercising at Long Bay Gaol. Photo courtesy of John Partridge, formerly of the Corrective Services.

Again, I just had to cop it sweet and behave myself. By this time World War 1 was in full swing. It was while I was in prison that I learnt that Ben had enlisted in the Australian Imperial Force. By the time I got that news, he had been sent to France so I could only wish him well and hope that he came home in one piece. The effect of the war on us was that we were put to knitting socks, sweaters and things for the boys who were overseas.

I did not worry about Kitty and Hedley because I was sure that Ben would have seen to it that they got part about his pay allotment.

This time my sentence expired in November, 1917. Once again I was free to go my own way. This felt marvellous! Unfortunately, I went back to the Bankstown area only to meet up with a man called John Fitzgerald. Thus began one of the worst periods in my life!

Fitz, as he was known, was, amongst other things, a cattle dealer but not a very honest one! He specialised in buying and selling stolen cattle. Fitz never asked questions of anyone who came to him with some faked receipt or some other bogus proof of purchase. Because he knew the animals were stolen he was able to buy them dirt cheap and sell them for a very nice profit. Of course, he did some genuine trading in animals to cover his shady sideline. It also helped to keep the coppers off his back.

Somehow, Fitz heard of my riding skills. He tracked me down and offered me a job moving cattle around for him. It seemed a stroke of luck to me then. It did not take me long to realise what he was doing but I turned a blind eye. I did not dob him in to the coppers because firstly, I was not a dobber anyway and secondly why should I do the coppers' dirty work for them?

The job itself was not much of a problem. All I had to do was help Fitz or some of his other riders move stock on to their new 'owners'. When stolen cattle were brought into his saleyards for sale there they did not stay long. Fitz would be itching to get them sold and out of his yards

97

before the coppers realised what was going on. At first, it puzzled me why the coppers did not seem to worry about what was going on, but I do not have to be a genius to figure that one out!

Some of the campfire gossip gave me some interesting information. One of the blokes told me that Fitz had done eighteen months hard labour in Bathurst Gaol for horse stealing. I think it was in 1906. Furthermore, he had an alias of Samuel Parker. Not that that means much. I do not know how many different names I have used over the years. Keeps the coppers busy trying to figure out who I really am.

I did not like Fitz as a person. He was a grubby individual who only washed when he thought of it and his clothes got even less attention. When he was sober he was friendly enough, which is how I came to be working for him in the first place. When he had had a few, watch out! He was ready to fight anyone or everyone. Generally, he preferred small blokes – or even women – to fight. Someone he could bash to a pulp was what he really liked.

At first, I would sometimes drop into his place and perhaps cook a meal for him. If we were driving some cattle I usually did the cooking there, too. That was all I ever did for him outside the droving. I wanted no part of him otherwise; only the money I got for helping him move the cattle.

Life in the circus had taught me to recognise that certain look in the eye when trouble was brewing, so I was always ready with my gun under my pillow. And I let Fitz know about it, too! Whenever we were out in the bush somewhere and I saw that look come into his eye, I would do a little practice target shooting just to warn him off. He got the message all right, but he did not like it one little bit. Tough! I might work for him but that was all.

That is not to say that he did not try it on a couple of times but a well-placed knee or a snap shot soon calmed him down. Fitz was the last man on earth I would choose to join me in a bit of nonsense.

I think if he had managed to get his way, I would have killed him and taken my chances with the law. I suppose it would have meant the hangman's rope if I was caught, but I think it would have been worth it. It never came to that, thank heavens!

Talking of violence, there was an old bloke called Chappie who worked for Fitz too. He had been with various circuses over the years until he got sick and had to give it up. He was doing odd jobs for Fitz when I met him. Chappie and I got on really well and we often had talks about the old days with the circuses and buckjumping shows, the people he had known there, somehow consoling each other for the good times that were gone. Chappie was a good bloke. I could never understand why he stuck with Fitz, but he seemed to actually admire that slob. Wonderful what will appeal to some people.

Fitz, on the other hand, would come home drunk and go over to have another beer with Chappie. Good old Chappie would oblige and then, for some reason or another, Fitz would get fighting mad and start belting Chappie. Chappie was only a little bloke and Fitz would really whale into him. You should have seen some of the bruises and even more serious injures I saw on Chappie. I did say Fitz was a 'nice' bloke! If I did not need the money I would have left Fitz long before that. Yet I don't know. How could I just up and go and leave Chappie to his mercy?

This particular time, I had been out moving some cattle on to their new 'owners'. When I got back to Fitz's after a day or so, I was dead beat and did not go around to Fitz like I usually did after a drive. Next morning, after I had given Fitz the money I had collected, I looked around and noticed that Chappie's gear had gone.

"Where's Chappie?" I demanded.

Fitz shrugged. "Gone," he said.

That was not good enough for me. "Gone where?" I persisted.

"How the hell do I know?" he snapped. "He just up and took off while I was away looking at some cattle. When I got back he was gone."

"Without saying goodbye to anyone or telling you where he was going?" I asked suspiciously. "Chappie wouldn't do that."

"I tell you he has just gone and that is all I know! He just up and left!" he spluttered at me.

It was then that I noticed Fitz's hands. They were swollen and bruised. He had been in a fight for sure. I smelt a rat. I knew he and Chappie had many a scrap in the past, but Chappie had never taken off before. Just patched himself up and gone on as usual. Could it be that Fitz had bashed Chappie up and this time it had gone too far? Maybe even killed Chappie. I shut up. I had to think.

I had been wary of Fitz for quite a while, but now I really watched him. My thought was that, if he had killed Chappie, there should be something around that would prove this and even lead me to where Chappie was – dead or alive. With that in mind, I started prowling around looking for something that would give me a clue.

I must have somehow let Fitz know what I was doing because he started watching me too. This was obvious by the way he kept sneaking looks at me when he thought I was not watching him. In fact, we were rather like a couple of dogs circling each other, looking for a weak point to attack.

If I had been smart, I would have left Fitz then and just disappeared somewhere. But I liked Chappie and just could not let the matter rest. I was convinced that Fitz knew a whole lot more about Chappie's disappearance than he was telling. Another thing was that I suddenly realised that I did not know Chappie's real name. In my world, names were not important and I had never asked what Chappie's correct name was. Why should I? He was just my friend, Chappie.

If I did not know his real name, how could I let his family know of my suspicions? With my record, I did not want to go to the police, but had thought that perhaps his family might decide to take matters into their own hands and call in the cops. I tried real hard to find his family or at least his real name but it was hopeless. Without a body or any means of identifying Chappie, what could I tell the cops?

Fitz could not let the matter rest either. Possibly because he could not afford to – at least that is how I saw what happened next. One day I answered a knock on the door of my place only to find two coppers there with a warrant for my arrest. That bastard, Fitz, had accused me of stealing one of his bloody cows. Well, if that was not the pot calling the kettle black I do not know what it was! It did not do me much good protesting that I had done no such thing. I was charged with the theft of his cow.

"Right, Mr Fitzgerald!" I thought. "I'll fix you!" By this time I had been released on bail so I grabbed my gun and headed straight for Fitz.

He must have got a shock when he saw me on his doorstep. There I was, angry as hell and worse still, armed! Fitz shrank back into the room and I followed him.

"What's all this shit about me stealing one of your cows?" I hissed?

"You know bloody well that you stole that black and white…" he started to bluster.

"Don't give me that! We both know that you are trying to make me back off about Chappie! You are afraid of what I might know and even worse of what I might do!"

Fitz had gone as white as a sheet at the mention of Chappie. "Chappie? What has Chappie to do with this?" he croaked. "You're mad!"

He was quite right. I was good and mad by this time – mad as hell, in fact. "You're afraid I might go to the coppers and tell them I think you have killed Chappie!" I spat at him.

Fitz glared at me for a few moments. I could almost hear him thinking how he could get around this one.

Finally he roared "With your record, do you think the coppers will believe you? A cock and bull story like that? No, of course not!" he sneered. "I don't know where Chappie is now and neither do you. Do you have a body to show the coppers? No, you don't. Nobody is going to listen to you unless there is a body so get out. Come back again and I will complain to the coppers that you are making a nuisance of yourself. They already have a complaint of stealing from me – how do you reckon another one will look?"

It was my turn to stop and think. At last I said real low and mean, "No, I do not know where Chappie's body is so perhaps the coppers will not listen to me – about Chappie, that is. But just you remember one thing. I do know a lot about your so-called business here. I can give the coppers names, dates and other information that they will find very interesting. Things like where you keep the cattle before passing them on to their new 'owners'. The coppers will love that! Your friends will not be very happy when the coppers start raiding them, either. Just think about that. Where will you be then? In prison, that's where!"

I had to stop for breath but I could see that I had rattled him. "However," I continued while he glared at me. "I will do a deal with you. Withdraw those charges of stealing and I will keep my mouth shut about Chappie and those oh so profitable little sidelines you have. I do not care how you do this – change your evidence, anything but just get it done! If you go on with those charges, I will see if I can do some sort of a deal with the coppers. I am sure they will be very interested in what I have to say. Even if I do finish up going to gaol for a while, you will be there for a much longer time! Yes, I will get out, but I will only stay out of your life if you get me off this charge. It is up to you, now."

With that I stamped out, slamming the door as I went. Still, I could not resist turning around and sending a few bullets into it just to help him think clearly. It took me a little longer to cool down enough to realise that I had made a big mistake! In my rage, I let Fitz know that I really believed that he had killed Chappie. If that was true and he really had killed Chappie, I could expect him to come after me in some way, probably with the intention of killing me too.

In his place, I would change my story and then maybe get rid of the one person who was at all likely to take an interest in Chappie's disappearance. I gathered my gear together and got out of there – fast.

Now, I had to find somewhere to stay that Fitz did not know about. He already knew about the McIntyres at Bankstown and would almost certainly look for me there. I could not go to Jean's when all those kids were there. I did not want to go to Kitty's with Hedley there. I picked up my gear and started walking.

CHAPTER SIX

THE TANGLED WEB

I see that I have neglected to keep up with what was happening with Kitty, Ben and Hedley so I suppose I should take a break here to tell you what went on with them during those years.

I have already told you that Ben started working with Prouds Ltd. which was a very well-known and well respected firm of jewellers located on the corner of Market and Pitt Streets in Sydney[151]. He was employed as a cleaner but, being Ben, he did his work well and kept his eyes open. I guess that it was here that he picked up many hints on making jewellery. He used this knowledge when he started making trinkets as a sideline to make more money for his new family.

Kitty was great when it came to running a house because she sure looked after her little family, managing their money quite well. In fact, what with Ben's jewellery making and Kitty's sewing bringing in added income

---

[151] According to a letter from Prouds Ltd dated October 5, 1929 and addressed to the Department of Repatriation Ben started working there in February, 1912. Prouds Ltd had a very good reputation for looking after their employees, particularly returned service men and women.

for them, they were really quite comfortably off. They certainly seemed very happy together.

It was the Nicol family that upset Kitty then.[152] They were very strict church-goers so they would have been shocked at the way Kitty's life was running off the rails. I think they looked on what Kitty was doing as nothing short of scandalous. First off, separating from Paul would have been bad enough, but to move in with Ben a year later and live with him as his wife!! This would have struck at the heart of their religious beliefs and the social standards of the day. Although I do not remember Kitty saying a word against them, I really believe the Nicols must have sort of disowned her.

In fact, I am not sure that she even attended the funeral of her father when he died in May, 1914.[153] Kitty was very proud of her father and the career he had carved out for himself after coming to Australia. Thinking back, I realise now that her Dad was as different as he could be from my Dad. For a start, he had a steady job and provided very well for his family. Something mine never did.

William had been born in Paisley in Scotland[154] but came to Australia aboard the *Norval,* arriving in Sydney in March 1880. By 1884 he had moved to Brisbane and was well enough established in his work to be able to send for his fiancée, Margaret Love. He married her soon after her arrival at the Presbyterian Church, Ann Street, Brisbane.[155] It was all rather sweet really. The couple moved to New South Wales before the birth of Kitty's older sister, Jean, who was born at Kiama in 1886[156]

---

[152]   The following is based on Christina's memories of her family as told to me as a child. I am sure that Christina was talking more to herself than to me when she told me about the Nicol family. DM

[153]   New South Wales Registration No. 6692/1914

[154]   Scottish Birth Certificate 000120

[155]   Information supplied by Christine Edwards, great grand-daughter of William Alexander Nicol.

[156]   New South Wales Birth Registration 25095/1886

and Kitty was born in Macquarie Street, Sydney, in July, 1890[157]. She was only two months older than me.

In between the births of the two girls they had moved to Sydney where William worked for the Manly Ferries for years. Kitty told me once that he had had a big say in the building of the *Bellubra*[158] which is still sailing around Sydney Harbour so I believe.

Poor Kitty never really knew her mother because she died when Kitty was only two years old.[159] After her death, William was left with two young children to care for so he finished up marrying his housekeeper, Hilda, in 1893.[160] Don't be shocked - needs must when the Devil drives, you know. They must have been happy because they had four children together.[161] It was the eldest of these, Willy, that Kitty was really fond of. She used to bend my ear telling me about their childhood together.

I think it was some time after he married Hilda that they moved to 100 Carabella Street, Kirribilli. Kitty used to tell me about how much she had loved to sit on the verandah of the home during the evening and look at the lights of Sydney. She really loved that city and never wanted to leave it.[162]

During the war years Kitty and I would sometimes sit around the fire and swap stories of our childhood. We were quite fascinated by each

---

[157] New South Wales Birth Registration 2037/1890
[158] Kitty often took me to Manly on this ferry and told me about her father's involvement in its construction
[159] New South Wales Death Registration 1605/1892
[160] New South Wales Marriage Registration 6702/1893
[161] William Hamilton Alexander 1627/1897; Hilda Elsie 3721/1904; Gleniffer 18001/1906 and Herbert Charles 18557/1908
[162] Christina would talk to me for hours about how beautiful the harbour was in those days. She always stressed that this was before The Bridge was built in 1932. DM

other's childhood and teenage years. One of Kitty's stories has really stuck in my mind over the years. We were sitting around the fire this night, drinking tea and eating some of Kitty's scones. She really knew how to make those scones. Light and fluffy with her homemade jam and whipped cream on top. Gorgeous. This night we were just idly talking away when she started to laugh.

"I don't know what has reminded me of this but what a laugh! You know how much I like to have a good old sing-song?"

I nodded. How I knew she liked to sing! She had the most awful singing voice, but would start singing at any time of day much to the anguish of those in earshot.[163]

"Well, this day I was sitting on the verandah, singing away when the next door neighbour yelled at me, 'Will you stop that racket? You sound like a cat sitting on a fence calling all the toms around!'

I sprayed crumbs all over the place! "What did you do?" I choked out through a mouthful of scone.

"Just laughed at him and went on singing. What I should have done was to invite him over to join the parade of tomcats! No, the poor man would probably have had a heart attack then." I still love that story and how typically Kitty it was.

When William died, he was the Superintending Engineer at the Port Jackson and Manly Steam Ship Company which owned the Manly Ferries.[164] A lot of the big nobs at the company, like managers and directors, came to the funeral as well as people from the Department of

---

163 This is another of the stories that Christina told me. I assume this happened before Paul Bellati entered her life. DM

164 New South Wales Death Registration No. 6692/1914 and Sydney Morning Herald May 15, 1914 Page 7.

Navigation. There were lots of members of the North Sydney Football Club there too because he had been vice-president there for years and years.

Not long after William's death, the Great War broke out. That really got the country in a flap. About June, 1915, Ben enlisted in the Australian Imperial Forces and was sent off to fight the Germans.[165] Well, he was English and I guess he felt some patriotic duty to go back and fight for the country of his birth. It was surprising though that, given his service in the Royal Navy, he did not join the navy, but perhaps he had no choice in the matter and simply went where he was sent. Ben had an honourable discharge from the Royal Navy so there was no reason for him to avoid enlisting in the Australian Navy. Come to think about it though, did Australia have a navy then?[166] I cannot remember the exact date that the Australian Navy really came into existence. I know they started out with ships borrowed from the Royal Navy. Be that as it may, Kitty would tell me about him when I visited her so I knew what was happening to him - at least, I knew a lot of what was happening to him.

Ben was sent to the 5th Machine Gun Company and embarked in Sydney on the *Argylshire* sometime in September, 1915.[167] First off, he was sent to Egypt for several months before going on to England. He pretty soon found himself in Etaples, France. From there it was a short step to the front. He must have impressed the officers over there because the Australian troops on the front line certainly did not think much of the English officers which, after Gallipoli, did not surprise me much.[168] It

---

[165] Australian Defence Records 2155 Series B2455. Ben enlisted on June 29, 1915

[166] In the years following Federation in 1901, Australia did not have a viable navy of her own but had to rely heavily on ships lent to her by the Royal Navy.

[167] Australian Defence Records (1914-1918) Series B2455 Item 2155 W8345

[168] It would have been hard to convince any member of the Australian Imperial Force that, on the whole, British officers were efficient either in the field or otherwise. These views flowed through to the civilian population on the servicemen's return. I had this from Arundel Pryor. DM

sounded like a smart kick in the pants would have done some of them a lot of good – the officers, I mean. I learned from some of the lads after they came home that the English and Australian officers were always arguing about something.[169]

One day I called on Kitty and she was in a fine old state. Ben had been seriously wounded at the Battle of Bullecourt on May 3, 1917.[170] The second Battle of Bullecourt, I mean, - there were two. Our 4th Divvy boys got so badly cut up in the first battle that there were not enough survivors to make up a fighting unit. It must have been terrible for the boys! No wonder so many came home absolute wrecks.

It took several weeks for reinforcements to come up and get them going again. Ben was injured on the first day of the second battle. When the War Department told Kitty about him being badly wounded she was in a panic. It seems that he had been shot twice in the chest so, yes, I guess you would call that serious.

Kitty said that Ben was evacuated to England but could not rejoin his unit until January, 1918. He copped it again in April, 1918, at some action in a place called Cachy Wood that was part of the Battle of Villers-Bretonneux.[171]

No wonder Kitty was so worried about Ben's injuries. Her half-brother, Willy, had been killed at Pozieres in 1916 (I cannot remember the exact date). Poor lad was only nineteen, too. As I have mentioned earlier, Kitty was very attached to Willy and for the rest of the time that I knew her,

---

[169]   Repatriation Records also show that Ben was slightly injured at Guedecourt in the battle of the Somme.

[170]   Australian Defence records (1914-1918) Series 2455 Item 2155 W8345 show that Ben received serious wounds at the Battle of Bullecourt. He was evacuated to England but was unable to rejoin his unit until January, 1918.

[171]   Repatriation Records Series C138/5 Item M57373 show this injury, but Ben described it as 'a mere scratch'. It still merited a mention in his records.

she would often speak of him with such sadness in her voice that it almost made me feel like crying too.[172]

When Ben enlisted in the Australian Imperial Forces in 1915, he had told the authorities that Kitty was his wife and that they had a son.[173] This is why Kitty was notified of his injuries when he was wounded. She rather hoped that he would be sent home or at least kept in England. But no! As soon as he was declared fit, back he went to the front, only to receive his third wound, one of the minor ones that he, himself, described as 'a scratch'.[174]

---

[172] Australian War Memorial Roll of Honour shows Willy's date of death as August 18, 1916 at the Battle of Pozieres. He was only nineteen when he died from wounds received.

[173] Australian Defence Records (1914-1918) Series 2455 Item 2155 W8345

[174] This is the one that he received in Cachy Wood

Hedley as a small child playing on his rocking horse.

As I have said, during those anxious war years, I would drop in from time to time – when I was not in gaol of course – to see Kitty and Hedley. I had to be careful because Hedley was getting old enough to start asking some difficult questions. Because Kitty and I were finding it difficult to answer these, it meant that I began to visit them less and less. Hedley was a cute kid but he could be a pain in the neck when he started asking questions and wanting answers too.

The bright side was that it would not be long before he was going to school. When that happened I would be able to see more of Kitty because he would be away at school during the day and not know whether I was visiting Kitty or not.

Also, from time to time Wally would call in and see me. How I enjoyed recalling the circus days with him! I heard from Hector occasionally, but I think his wife, Florrie, did not like him contacting me. I think she frowned on me because of the way I spoke. Well, what could she expect? I really did not have much education. Coupled with that I had a short temper with the result that I could talk like a bullocky when I felt like giving someone a stir.[175]

Getting back to my story now, when all that trouble blew up with Fitz, I knew I had to find a another place to stay very quickly. Going to the McIntyres in Bankstown would not do because I had told Fitz about them so that would probably be the first place he would look for me. Silly of me to tell him, but one cannot see into the future.

---

[175] This has been suggested by some members of the Hunt family. Unfortunately, this is oral history and cannot be proven.

Kitty, her sister Jean and Jean's two daughters and Jessie.

I did think to ask Jean to let me stay with her, but I knew Jack did not like me much and in any event, there were lots of kids there now. Jean certainly made up for Kitty's lack of children! For sure, I could not stay with Kitty.

I eventually found a tumble down place which would do me for the time being until I was able to arrange something better. The trouble was that I still had to eat so I started stealing whatever I needed to keep body and soul together. I had learnt a lot during my days on the road, things like shop-lifting and 'finding' bags and trifles carelessly left lying about. The food I stole I kept for myself but anything else I found I sold to get some money.

I laid as low as possible because I was still worried about Fitz and what he would do if he found me. He would still be very angry with me. I knew he would be plotting and planning, looking for some sort of vengeance – I could not put enough money on that one.

One day he saw me at Central Railway Station in Sydney and the look he gave me! If looks could kill, I would have dropped dead there and then.[176] When he started to head towards me I panicked and ran down some nearby stairs and on to another platform where a train was just pulling into the station. I lost him, thank heavens, but it shook me up. Too close, by half, for me.

I even stopped visiting Kitty so much because I was scared he would follow me home and heavens knows what he would do then! Still, I HAD kept my part of the bargain with him. I just wished I could be sure that he would do the same with his part of the bargain. He always did fight dirty.

---

[176]   This story is oral history but it could well have happened as told here. Sydney's Central Railway Station was a very busy place and Fitz and Jess may well have caught sight of each other.

Hedley in a small copy of the Australian Imperial Forces
uniform. He is aged about six or seven in this photo

When the war ended in November, 1918, Kitty looked forward to Ben coming home to her, but to her disappointment, he was not to get back to Australia until mid-1919.[177] It was Arundel who got back to Australia first and immediately called on Kitty. Now let me see; that would have been around December, 1918 or perhaps January 1919 and the very first thing he did on landing was to go and visit Kitty.[178]

He had always been keen on her and kept writing to her when he was in the Middle East with the Australian Light Horse – even sent her presents. I remember a lovely moonstone necklace and ear-rings set which had the moonstones set in eighteen carat gold.[179] He missed out on the famous Light Horse charge at Beersheba, which I was told was the last great cavalry charge in history. He was in hospital when that happened and missed his moment of glory – or perhaps he missed out on being killed.[180]

I would meet Arundel sometimes when I visited Kitty and I did not have to be a genius to see he was head over heels in love with her. As for Kitty, she was just not interested in Arundel – it was Ben that she wanted.

It was somewhere around then that the Spanish Flu struck Sydney. What a panic it caused! Some people blamed the soldiers who were coming home then, but I think that was a bit rough on them. However it got to Australia and it sure stirred things up. Kitty said that she had read that somewhere between fifty and one hundred thousand people died in the world. Just think 40% of Sydney's population got the flu

---

[177] Australian Defence Records B2455 Item 2155

[178] Australian Defence Records B2455 Item 1216. Arundel was invalided home December 22, 1918 aboard the Leicestershire.

[179] Sadly the ear-rings have been lost but the necklace remains and has become a family heirloom. DM

[180] Australian Defence Records B2455 Item 1216

and over four thousand of them died![181] The strange thing was that it seemed to prefer young, healthy people. I remember that they set up emergency hospitals at Sydney Showground and the Deaf, Dumb and Blind Institution as well as other places that I forget. The regular hospitals could not take so many sick people and these were pretty much makeshift hospitals. There were even undergraduate medical students handing out medicine and advice.[182] The panic even closed the Sydney University.[183]

Kitty was very worried about Hedley getting the flu and he had to wear a sort of mask to keep the germs out. Well, so did everyone else so that was no big deal. While all this was going on Kitty was making her plans which included petitioning for a divorce from Paul Bellati in July, 1919 on the grounds of desertion.[184] Well, she missed out there because Paul counter-petitioned for a divorce on the grounds of adultery.[185]

Kitty based her petition on the fact that Paul had gone to America for a while soon after they had separated sometime in 1911 or 1912. She also petitioned for sole custody of Hedley, but wanted Paul to support them both. What a hope! Even I could see that Paul would never even acknowledge Hedley as his son; much less would he ever even dream of supporting them both.

I think Kitty's reason for all this was that she hoped that Ben would marry her when he came back to Australia and she was clearing the way for him to do just that. To support her petition she asked me to be witness to her having lived with Paul until sometime in 1912 and that Hedley was his baby. I was glad to do her this favour after all she had

---

[181] 'An Australian perspective of the 1918-1919 Influenza Pandemic', *NSW Public Health Bulletin* Vol 17; No. 7-8 p.103

[182] *Dr. John Cawley Madden, The Cawley Madden Family Chronicle 'His life and Times*

[183] Report of the Senate 1919 *University Calender 1920*

[184] Petitioner: Christina Margaret Bellati Divorce 628/1919

[185] Petitioner: Paul Bellati Divorce 731/1919

done for me. So I lied. Big deal. I signed the statement as Elizabeth McIntyre just so that I would not be connected with Jessie McIntyre. Good thinking, eh?[186]

Ben sailed for Australia on the *Yiringa* and Kitty and Hedley were on the wharf to meet him when it sailed into Sydney Harbour about June or July, 1919.[187] I did not go because I was not that interested in seeing him again. So they could have him all to themselves. This seemed to be the right thing for me to do. It must have been a happy reunion! It came as no surprise – to me at least – that Kitty and Ben made up for lost time, if you know what I mean![188]

Paul was obviously keeping an eye on Kitty and what she was doing because he was quick to counter-sue on the grounds of adultery naming Ben as the co-respondent. Paul was able to bring evidence that Ben and Kitty had committed adultery in July 1919 at various places around Sydney.[189] I forget the places he named but there were at least three.

He also had witnesses to support his claim that he was not living with Kitty when Hedley was conceived so he could not possibly be the father of the baby. With all the evidence he had and all the witnesses he found, it looked as if he would have no trouble in getting his divorce with Kitty being the guilty party. Evidently the court found that he was not the father of Hedley either, because he was not required to provide maintenance for Hedley.

---

[186] Divorce Record 731/1919. Christina was trying to defend herself against Paul's claims of adultery.

[187] Christina told me that she took my father to see his father come home from the war. I thought she mean Arundel and it was not until I started the research for this book that I realised she did not meant Arundel – she meant Ben.

[188] Two places named for where the adultery took place were the Burlington Hotel, Hay Street, Sydney and 108 Glenmore Road, Paddington. Divorce Records 638 and 731/1919

[189] Paul's divorce papers claimed that "…and other places in and around Sydney in New South Wales."

I happened to drop in on Kitty one day when Ben was there. It was about this time that Ben got his nickname of 'Major'. He had always had a very military sort of bearing right from when I first met him when I was part of Martini's Buckjumpers, but after the Great War it was even more obvious. His friends started calling him 'The Major' and it stuck. Ben rather liked it and began acting up to the name. Actually, Ben never was a major in any army – British or Australian[190]. The officers in the British Army would have died rather than have the son of a farm labourer become an officer in their army. The mere thought would probably have reduced them to a quivering jelly.[191] According to what our boys said when they came home after the war, the British army (lower ranks, of course) paid a terrible price in casualties because of this stuck up attitude.

There I go again, getting side tracked. Since Paul was suing for a divorce, Kitty and Ben must have decided it would be better if they did not live together until after the divorce was sorted out. In spite of this, Ben would drop in to see Kitty and Hedley.[192] It was only a happy get-together over a cup of tea and biscuits, so Kitty said.

Things were very friendly, in fact. One day Ben was telling me about some of his wartime experiences which were really quite interesting – horrible in some ways but interesting nevertheless - it dawned on me that there was that old gleam in his eye, but what really struck me was that he was looking at me, not Kitty.

In amongst all this divorce fuss, a letter from the Department of Army arrived for Ben. It contained a copy of a letter from some woman in

---

190 I hold the Governor General's official parchment confirming Ben's appointed to the office of lieutenant as from 22nd April, 1917. I have yet to find any evidence that he claimed he became a Major and challenge anyone who does claim this to produce their supporting evidence.DM

191 This came from Wally Craven via Jim McJannett's notes of discussion and interviews with Wally about Jess.

192 This came from Wally Craven via Jim McJannett's notes on discussions and interviews about Jessie.

France called Olympe Marchand. At the time he did not say anything about this to me but later he told me about it. The letter had been sent to the army and forwarded by them to him. Olympe claimed that he had promised to marry her, but said that he had to return to Australia before he could be discharged from the army. She claimed he had promised that, when he was demobbed from the army, he would go back to France and marry her.[193]

Ben never answered her letters although she made several more attempts to find him through the army. Poor thing, it must have been hard for her when the army wrote to her saying that when Ben enlisted in 1915 he had a wife and son living in Australia.

Let me tell you this. Wally always said that Ben was great company and could charm a bee from the honey pot. Perhaps he charmed her into getting pregnant and that was why she was so insistent about finding him. Just a guess but it sounds like it.[194]

Now I do not know if Ben ever told Kitty about Olympe but I reckon he probably did. Kitty was very much in love with Ben and if she did know about Olympe it would have hurt her dreadfully. Ben never mentioned anything about that; neither did Kitty. She had her pride, did Kitty.

In the meantime, Ben and I were seeing each other and it was not long before he was pushing me to marry him. Poor Kitty! We really did pretty bad by her. It all went to prove what a charmer Ben was. Olympe, Kitty, me and I do not know how many other girls!

He even charmed me to the altar!

---

[193]   Olympe Marchand wrote several letters to the Australian Department of the Army during 1919 and 1920. These letters are in his Australian Defence Records B2455 Item 2155

[194]   Jim McJannett's notes. Wally often referred to Ben as a good mate but he was also a ladies' man and a very smart dresser. A real charmer, in fact.

I never admired Kitty as much as I did when we told her we were getting married.[195] I insisted on telling her before the wedding although Ben wanted to leave it until afterwards. We called on her one afternoon and over tea and biscuits we made the announcement. As it happened, Arundel was there too, but we still went ahead and told Kitty.

You should have seen her! Her face just went blank. She took a sip of tea and then nibbled a biscuit before saying anything. You have to hand it to her – she was a lady through and through!

"That is really good news!" she said finally. "When is the big day?"

Ben looked a bit sheepish so I thought I had better step in here.

"December 11, at St. Peters Church of England, Richmond," I answered as calmly as I could. I did not have the nerve to ask her to the wedding or to be my Matron of Honour or anything like that. I glanced at Arundel but he was only looking really surprised. As I looked, his eyes suddenly brightened and he was all attention.

"Well, congratulations to you both," she smiled. "It is my turn to give you a surprise now. Arundel and I have something to tell you; we are going to beat you to the altar. We will be married in a couple of weeks!" She fidgeted for a minute then went on. "It will be a very quiet wedding as we do not want anything too fussy." I'll bet they didn't!

But you should have seen Arundel's face! It went from being startled and worried to the face of one very happy man! He jumped up and put his arm around Kitty.

---

[195] The ensuing scene is a product of my imagination but I am sure something very similar did happen. I knew Christina intimately – she practically reared me – and she would never have made a fuss about something no matter how hurt she was. I have put this knowledge into Jessie's comment. DM

"Well, well. How about that?" he stuttered. I do not know who was the most surprised – Arundel, Ben or me!

I looked at Kitty but she did not have the face of a happy bride. It was the face of a stone statue. I think she may have been trying not to cry. Ben and I left soon afterwards.

We later heard that Kitty and Arundel had married at the Redfern District Registrar's Office.[196] I cannot remember seeing Kitty or Hedley again. They just went out of my life. For days after that visit to Kitty one of her favourite sayings kept ringing in my ears.[197] See what you think. It is easy to remember,

"Oh, what a tangled web we weave
When first we practise to deceive".

I think a bloke called Robbie Burns wrote it.

Ben and I married as planned at St. Peters Church of England in Richmond, New South Wales, on December 11, 1920.[198] What a fool I was! I should never have married him. Deep down, I already knew that. Poor Ben! I was the worst possible wife for him.

Looking back now, it would have been better if I had married Arundel, but he only had eyes for Kitty. Arundel and I were alike. We both loved the bush and had a complete disregard for the man-made laws which seemed to both of us to be a complete waste of time. On the other hand, Kitty and Ben were made for each other as they both wanted a domestic life in the city. What a joke! Arundel falling for Kitty; Kitty falling for Ben and Ben falling for me who did not give a damn for either Arundel

---

[196] New South Wales Marriage Registration 15999/1920. This was a bigamous marriage as Paul had not yet finalised the divorce between himself and Christina.

[197] Christina was a great one for sayings and quotations. This was one of her favourites. DM

[198] New South Wales Marriage Registration 16592/1920

or Ben. It could almost be a case of Fate playing some cynical game in an effort to mess up our lives.

Now the interesting bit about all this is that Kitty's divorce from Paul had not been properly finalised in 1920 when she married Arundel.[199] In which case this new marriage of hers was bigamy! I had to laugh at the neat way she had turned the table on Ben and me. In later years, Jean told me that the divorce did not become absolute until 1925 because Paul kept putting off applying for matters to be finalised. Probably a bit of revenge on his part. I never said anything at the time because I was feeling a bit guilty and anyway it was none of my business if they really did commit bigamy. Let the coppers do their own dirty work, I say! Neither Ben nor I were dobbers.

It was very sad but after that I did not see Kitty again. She and Arundel married and had a happy life together so Jean had told me.[200] Hedley had a good education, too. Kitty would have seen to that. Did I mention that Arundel was a plumber? Well, he was. After Hedley left school, he served his apprenticeship with Arundel and went on to become a plumber too. So you see, I really did Hedley a good turn when I gave him up to Kitty to be her own son.

Jean, good friend that she is, kept me informed on how things were going with Kitty and Hedley. I was genuinely interested, you know, but I was sure they would be better left to make their own lives without me messing things up for them. It seems I have quite a talent for doing that. I really do love them both, you know but, still, it is very nice to hear occasionally how they were going, particularly Hedley.

---

[199] It has been argued that Christina did not realise that the divorce was not yet final. In which case, why did she give her name as 'Glen Nicol' and her birthplace as Paisley, Scotland if she was not trying to conceal her true identity?

[200] Following the divorce becoming absolute, Christina and Arundel lawfully married at the Methodist Church, Newtown. This time Christina gave her correct name, birthplace and marital status. At last they had a legal marriage. New South Wales Marriage Registration 7160/1926

I never did know if Kitty had noticed what was going on between Ben and me, but I think she must have suspected something. Perhapsd she was just hoping that it would all blow over and Ben would eventually marry her. I wonder if she ever knew about Olympe Marchand. Whatever she knew or suspected, Ben and I hurt her very badly and I am sorry that it all cost me a good friend.

CHAPTER SEVEN

FRESH AIR AND FREEDOM

Ben and my wedding was very quiet too. I had Mum as my witness and a Mr. Douglass was the witness for Ben. I did not know Mr. Douglass but he seemed a nice bloke. Mum made me a wedding dress which I liked very much. I hardly knew myself in it and it felt very strange after my riding pants. Ben said I looked beautiful so I guess he was happy.[201]

I did not have a bridesmaid. I would have liked to have had Kitty as Matron of Honour, but that was just not possible under the circumstances. Although Kitty had not told me when they planned to marry, Jean said they married at the District Registrar's Office, Redfern on November 26, 1920.[202]

Ben and I settled down to married life in a house in Yurong Street in the city.[203] At least Ben settled down. Ben had been lucky because Prouds gave him back his job as a cleaner in spite of his war wounds – something a lot of bosses did not do - and how these wounds affected him and his

---

[201] The following chapters are largely based on oral history but I have given references wherever possible. DM

[202] New South Wales Marriage Registration No. 15999/1920

[203] Divorce Records 1472/1927

breathing. Prouds kept him on until at least 1929. I lost sight of him afterwards and so I do not know what happened to him after, but I expect Prouds kept him on the payroll as long as they could.[204]

He never said anything about it to me, but I think he made enquiries about getting Hedley from Kitty. If he tried to get Hedley back, it would have made the Great War look like a minor skirmish. Kitty would have fought him tooth and nail. I think Ben was looking to get Hedley made legitimate. Well, he came a thud. We never did get Hedley, thank heavens.[205]

In his pre-war days with Prouds, he had watched the craftsmen design and create expensive jewellery and learnt quite a bit about their way of doing things. When he went back to his job after the war, he kept an eye out for anything he could learn. Don't get me wrong. He never skimped on his work. Ben was not like that. He just kept his eyes open while he did his cleaning work. So the quality of the jewellery he produced improved to the standard where he was able to have a nice little sideline in his time off.

When we married he gave his occupation as a jeweller but I expect he felt that sounded better than cleaner.[206] It was hard enough for us to manage on a cleaner's wages as it was, so the extra he made from selling his jewellery was very welcome. Pretty little trinkets were what sold best but he really liked what he called scrimshaw. This was a sort of carving of bones or for the more expensive version, of ivory. I think that is where Ben learnt to carve scrimshaw because that was what some of the sailors did in their spare time on board ship.

---

[204]   Prouds Ltd letter to the Department of Repatriation dated May 10, 1929

[205]   If this was Ben's aim, his application would have failed. The law at that time only approved a child being made legitimate if there was some legal bar to the parents marrying by the time of birth. There was no bar to the marriage of Jessie and Ben when Hedley was born in 1913 because they were both over the age of twenty one and single.

[206]   New South Wales Marriage Registration No. 16592/1920

I was expected to stay at home and be a good little housewife. Ben would have loved and protected me from the difficulties and dangers of life. He never did realise that they were the breath of life to me. The thrill of pitting yourself against a buckjumping horse or bullock; the dangers and unexpected challenges of the bush drew me like a magnet. How I wish I could still enjoy them.

But the marriage never really worked. Oh, I know Ben loved me and did his best to make me happy, but it was no use. We were too different. Don't get me wrong – Ben was a good bloke and I am sure he and Kitty would have been happy together because they were so alike. It was just his bad luck that he fell for me. As I have said several times, the settled domestic life was not for me. I am more certain than ever that I got it right when I gave Hedley to Kitty, but Ben could not see it that way. I now know that it was one of the few big decisions in my life that I did get right.

I was the problem in the marriage. Ben wanted to live in the central part of Sydney, close to his work and the city life. As for me – well, talk about a square peg in a round hole! All I wanted was to be in the bush or as near to it as I could get. During the war I had managed to be settled enough with the McIntyres at Bankstown, because Bankstown had plenty of open land and farms so I did not feel shut in. Of course, those enforced stays at Long Bay Gaol did not help but what I really wanted – indeed, needed – was to be where there was plenty of space and fresh air where I could be my own person and have my horses.

But the society back then did not see it that way. Women were expected to look after the men, have the babies and bring them up to be replicas of themselves. If a woman was lucky, she got a good bloke who looked after her and their children, but there were plenty of women too who were not so lucky. They were the ones who got bashed by the drunken sods of husbands but never complained. They even hid the bruises and broken bones because they were too afraid to do anything else. In my opinion, what they should have done was to just walk out on their husband. That type never change so why should a woman put up with that for the rest of her – possibly short life?

I was one of the lucky ones because Ben was not like that. I was the problem. I could ride as well or better than most men; I was a very good shot; I could fight like a tiger if needed but I was a woman! I had to be shielded and protected from the harsh winds of life. What a laugh!

Add to that that I am a damned good bushman – possibly one of the best. Ask anyone around here; even the police know how good I am and all the trouble I gave them when they tried to arrest me. I have stolen plenty of cattle from the farms around here and gotten away with it right under the noses of both owners and coppers. All due to my skills in the bush. If I disappear into the bush or into my cave I defy anyone to find me.

James (Jimmy) McDonald, Police tracker, was a friend of Jessie. Despite this friendship, he was a much liked and well respected resident of the Kandos area. Photo Courtesy of Des Honeysett.

I learnt much of this from my Aboriginal friends around here. It is those same Aboriginals who have looked after me and helped me when I had my black spells.[207] All they saw was someone in need and I am so grateful to them for their care.

Kitty was another rebel - even her sister described her as the wild one of the family. Kitty often said that anything a man could do, a woman can do as well if not better.[208] No wonder we got on so well. I remember the fuss in her family when she got her driver's licence.[209] It was 1910 when car drivers had to have a licence. Kitty was one of the first women in New South Wales to get her licence and very proud of it she was too! And what a to-do it caused with her family. It was unwomanly to drive a car. That was for the men who knew so much more about these matters. She was still with Paul then, but I suspect it was one of the many things that caused their split.

It seemed strange to me that anyone would prefer to drive an automobile when they could ride horses. Messing around with a lot of levers, knobs, pedals and other mysterious things could not compare with the friendship, loyalty and mobility that a horse can give you.

You can imagine the family's horror the first time Kitty lit up a cigarette in front of them![210]

I thought it quite odd that Ben liked both of us so much. He was the kind of a bloke who wanted to settle down and have kids. He had a roving eye all right and his wife would have to put up with that, but that was fine with me. I had had plenty of blokes, but none of them came up to what I wanted. They never seemed to see me as their equal.

---

[207] As told by Col Ribeaux of Capertee

[208] This was one of Christina's favourite sayings. DM

[209] Christina was very proud of this and frequently boasted about it to me in later years. The Rayner family remember the horror of their parents when Christina got her licence. DM

[210] I do not know when Christina started smoking but it was probably sometime during the 1920s. DM

The wild and mountainous country near Jessie's hut in Widden Valley. Photo courtesy of Greg Powell.

Regional Map of the Kandos/Rylstone area showing the Wollemi National Park and Nullo Mountain. Photo courtesy of Mid Western Regional Council, Mudgee

Still, with the fear of what Fitz would do if he caught up with me, I thought it worth a go with Ben. I soon learned my mistake! Ben's place in Yurong Street, right in the heart of Sydney was the last place on earth that I wanted to be although that, together with the change of name, did provide somewhere for me to hide from Fitz for a while.

Soon after our wedding I started taking trips to visit Hector at his place in Kandos. I loved that area with its rugged mountains, hidden valleys, blue skies, glorious colours and wildlife. My dream then was to have a place of my own somewhere in that Rylstone/Kandos area where I could live in peace and look after my horses. The loneliness would not worry me. I have been lonely ever since Martini's played its final night.

It was on one of my rambles through the mountains that I stumbled on Widden Valley and immediately fell in love with it.[211] The hills were honeycombed with caves while on three sides the valley was closed in by sandstone peaks rising up to three thousand feet and forming part of the most eastern fall of the Great Dividing Range. The entrance to the valley in the north was hidden by hillocks covered with low brush and scrubland although some of the land had been cleared for pasture.

---

[211] In the 1960s Jenifer Ellis and husband Cliff lived on a property that encompassed where Jessie's farm and hut had been. This is her description of the valley.

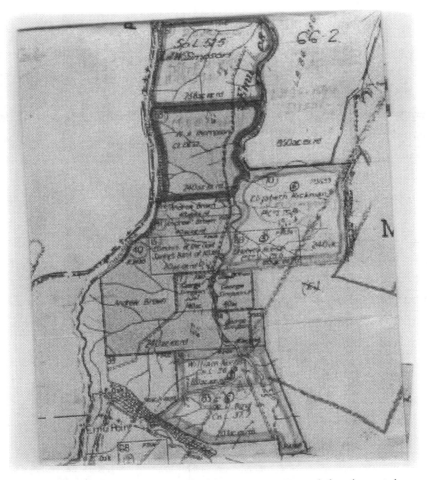

Map of Widden Valley landholdings. Note Jessie's land on right.
Map courtesy of Land and Property Management Authority

It did not take much effort to imagine why the first settlers to come into this beautiful valley had a tough time getting to the valley floor. They probably would only have had a bullock dray to carry their belongings along the rough bush tracks to the escarpment and then make their way down the steep slope over boulders and low undergrowth, through tall cedar groves covered with bush orchids. It must have been a beautiful place then – it still is – but what a journey!

There were a few graves of the early settlers down by the creek. When I visited this small cemetery, it was sheltered by old elms; a place of utter peace. No wonder I fell in love with it! This was where I desperately wanted to get some land and settle down. I have never regretted that decision for one minute.

After finding this haven of beauty and peace, you can imagine how hard it was for me to come back to the noise and confined spaces of inner Sydney. I hated it. Gradually I slipped into the habit of spending more and more time at Hector's place, slipping away to visit my dream valley, and paying less and less attention to Ben.[212] It was not long before we were quarrelling furiously about my trips. I simply could not give them up and Ben wanted me to have another baby. No, thanks!

Hector had married a lass called Florence Carney in Brewarrina in June,[213] 1913 and they had a son, Kenneth Archibald Hugh, the following year. In later years, a lot of people thought that young Ken was my son. For the record, he was a year younger than Hedley and most definitely not my son. I often wondered if Hector or Florrie heard these rumours and if they did, what they thought about them. They never said anything and I never asked them. If they did hear those silly rumours, I hoped they found them as funny as I did.

---

[212] From Ben's point of view, Jessie wanted more and more money from him while she spent less and less time with him. It is unknown if Jessie started her 'nest egg' about this time – money from cattle duffing.

[213] New South Wales Marriage Registration 10379/1913

Hector and Florrie had a fine lot of children; Kenneth, of course, in 1914; Florence Jessie in 1916 (known as Jessie); Jack Patrick in 1918; Margaret Katherine (known as Kit) in 1921; Elsie Sylvia in 1925 and Daphne May in 1927. After all this time I cannot remember the exact dates but those were the years, right enough.

Florrie was the midwife around town and must have brought many of the district's babies into the world. Doctors were few and far between in the country then so women in rural areas often had to rely on the local midwife to look after them during their confinement. Florrie must have found it a handful to manage a husband and so many of her own children as well as their home, without being called out at odd hours to deliver a baby! Still she seemed to manage it all OK.

I do not think she liked me much because she disapproved of my way of life. She probably thought I should settle down with Ben and have a family. I had told Hector about Hedley, but I do not know if he told Florrie. I certainly did not tell her, mainly because I did not think it any of her business. She never mentioned it, but she may have guessed. Still, she was always welcoming whenever I dropped by to see them all.

I must admit that I liked young Ken who was close to Hedley's age. In fact, he was really my favourite. I liked to play with him when he was little, teaching him things to do when he got older, like riding. But I always liked the feeling of handing him back to Florrie even when he was older. No permanent children in my life thank you!

During one of my visits to Hector and Florrie, I met a bloke called Andy Black.[214] Actually, Andy was not his real name – I think that was George. His family had been in the area for a very long time[215] and Andy was a

---

[214] George Albert Andrew Black New South Wales Birth Registration No.28169/1887, popularly known as Andy Black.

[215] Father – William; Mother – Elizabeth New South Wales Birth Registration 28169/1887

true bushie! Later, my neighbour in Widden Valley Bremmer Morrison, said that Andy was a superb horseman who knew the Nullo like the back of his hand. Andy could, and often did, move cattle on the blackest of nights but never got lost. Andy was completely at home in the bush.

I agree! Andy was what I would call a terrific bushman. And pretty good at stealing cattle and horses too. It did not take long for us to become friends and when Andy discovered how good I was in the saddle and my attitude to other people's property, we soon started doing a few jobs together. I tried to keep this from Hector and Florrie but I think they got pretty suspicious about what was going on.

After that brush with Fitz, I had laid low trying not to attract the coppers' attention. I liked getting my share of the money from the cattle we stole and this made me more and more daring. Andy knew the bush better than anyone else I knew and, best of all, he did not object to teaching me some of his tricks. His knowledge of the mountains was unbelievable. He knew all the hidden tracks, highways and byways, caves where you could hide, valleys where you could hide the stolen cattle until you were ready to take them to the saleyards. On top of all this, he was a first class rider. He could find his way through the mountains on the blackest of nights without a mishap.[216] Was it any wonder that I learnt as much as I could from him?

Eventually, I gave up running backwards and forwards between Kandos and Sydney or staying with Hector and Florrie to move in with Andy at his place at Summervale. Summervale was in a good position as far as I was concerned. A very steep rather inaccessible road wound up through high timber country to this pretty little place in a tiny valley on top of the plateau. About six farms of about twelve hundred acres nestled there. It was a beautiful spot![217]

---

[216] Bremmer Morrison's Memoirs
[217] Ian Buckley, *Journal of the Stockmen's Hall of Fame*, Longreach. March, 1993 Issue

If any unwelcome visitors, such as coppers, came towards the place I could see them coming a mile off. This meant that I could scarper off and disappear into the hills without the visitors knowing any different. Not that we had much trouble with the coppers then. But still, there are times you do not want visitors and visitors you do not want to see. So it was all for the best.[218]

If it was the coppers coming I could go off over the basalt cliff face, into its nooks and crannies and no-one would have a chance of finding me then. One has to be cautious, you know. By the way, to satisfy convention I was said to be Andy's housekeeper. I was his housekeeper all right but there were added benefits, too!

There were some pretty wild tales going around about our not-so-lawful activities. We encouraged these, even added to them when we could, in an effort to keep people away. One tale I remember was told to me by a bloke called Taylor. It seems that Andy had some stolen cattle hidden in one of the isolated valleys or hollows as they were called.

The one that Andy was in at the time was at the top of Widden Valley. It had high rock walls, a narrow entrance and was said to have been a favourite hideout for the bushranger, Thunderbolt. While Andy was resting the cattle he got word that the police were headed his way. To avoid being charged with the theft of the cattle, Andy is supposed to have shot the cattle and beat a hasty retreat out of the valley. I asked Andy about that but he just grinned and said, "Some people will believe anything." Maybe they did but I still cannot make up my mind about that one.

In one of my rambles through the bush, I spotted this strange overhang of rock that had a young tree growing right beside it. It was well up a very steep rock face and the tree seemed to be hanging onto the rock face for

---

218 *Journal of the Stockmen's Hall of Fame*, Longreach. March, 1993 issue

dear life. I do not know what made me do it - curiosity, I guess – but I decided to take a closer look.[219]

What a climb! I was hot and sweaty by the time I got there but it was worth it. I found small ledge leading into a cave. The young tree that I had noticed actually screened the entrance to the cave. Of course, I had to look into the cave and discovered that it was quite a large cave which, with a few comforts added, could make a very comfortable hideout. The approach was so steep that I doubted a horse could get up there. Even if he did make it, the downward climb would have a very good chance of disaster. This did not bother me because a horse could be hidden in the scrub somewhere nearby. There were plenty of hidey-holes for a horse.

I was particularly pleased with the way one could look out over the valleys and hills because you could see for miles and know if anyone was coming.

"What a great place to hide!" was my first thought. "All I need are a few things to make me warm and comfortable and I could hide here for months if necessary. Nobody would be able to find me unless I chose to tell them. What a find!"

I then set about taking a few things up to the cave. Just creature comforts like an old cupboard made of wooden crates, a bed and an old mattress, an old chair, knives and forks, plates and, of course, a good billy! When the weather started getting colder I made myself a wagga.[220] With all that, I figured I should be as snug as a bug in a rug.

Looking back, I have to laugh at all the trouble that bed caused! I persuaded Andy to give me hand with it. He did not like the idea of my taking things to the cave because he could not see any point to doing that.

---

[219]   This version of how Jessie discovered her cave is the product of my imagination but it seems reasonable to assume that something like this did happen. DM

[220]   A wagga was a rug of two pieces of material sewn together and then stuffed with odd scraps of material and wool or whatever could be used to keep the owner warm.

It was hard enough convincing him to help me but the climb getting that damned bed up to the cave was appalling. How I wished that one of us had Ben's skills as a rigger! It would not have taken Ben long to figure out a way to get that bed up to the cave but in the end Andy and I did manage to do just that, despite Andy's moaning about women's crazy ideas.

When I made up the bed and set up the cupboard, the cave looked a safe and comfortable hideout which was to prove very handy later on.

It was not long after I found the cave that Andy decided to get out of "Summervale" and move to a place called "Thalgoona" which was not very far from my cave either! This made me feel very safe, indeed. At the first hint of trouble, I could disappear into the bush and hide in my cave indefinitely.

As I spent more and more time in the Kandos area, Ben became more and more annoyed with me. Eventually, he wrote me a letter in early 1924 because I was spending so much time there and he was seeing very little of me.[221] Basically, he said he would send me money until the first of June. After that, if we did not come to some acceptable understanding about me coming back to live with him, he would not send me any more money or accept any responsibility for my debts. He then finished with "Your affectionate husband, Ben." Huh! What a joke! And I thought he was one man I could depend on.

Oh, for Mart. He would have understood and helped me! I did not even bother to answer Ben's letter.

Now that I had this established relationship with Andy, I was able to get some money for myself. I stretched this out by stealing such things as food, clothing and a few odds and ends particularly for my cave. For some reason, I have stuck with my married name, Hickman. Of course,

---

221   A copy of this letter is included in the Divorce 1472/1927 file.

from time to time I have been forced to use an alias, but even in court I remained Jessie Hickman.

Let me see if I can remember some of the names I have used. Yes, there was McIntyre, of course, but I never really regarded that as an alias because it was Mum's maiden name. Some of the others were Mrs. Bell, Mrs. Payne,[222] Mrs. Hudson, G Murray and Jessie Glen Thomas.[223] There were others but I cannot recall them all now.

Andy and I moved out of Summervale and settled in Thalgoona, a property that Andy had not too far away. A lot of the properties around there were leased so I do not know whether Andy actually owned Summervale or just leased it. The same goes for Thalgoona. Anyway, we moved from Summervale to Thalgoona. The good part of this is that Thalgoona was close to my cave too so I could still head for it if I felt the need to.

It was during those exciting days that the great race occurred. Automobiles were being used quite a bit more although only the more wealthy farmers could afford them. There was a bloke – I think he was called Dunn – who had a shiny, brand new T-model Ford that he was very proud of. So proud in fact, that he issued a challenge to anyone mounted on a real four-legged horse to race him and his automobile up the mountain.

That was too much for me! I accepted the challenge. I was sure I could win if they did not put too many rules on the race – particularly any rule about sticking to the same track as the automobile took. Andy took me at my word that I would win and started placing bets wherever he could find someone to give him decent odds. When Mr Dunn turned up for

<hr />

[222] Mrs Bell and Mrs Payne are given as aliases in Prison File 13150;
[223] Miss G Murray, New South Wales Police Gazette March 6, 1918 Page 114; Mrs. Hudson New South Wales Police Gazette August 15, 1928 Page 529 and also Jessie Glen Thomas also in the New South Wales Police Gazette August, 15, 1928 Page 529.

the race, we found that he had a passenger and there were several bags of something in the back of the Ford.[224]

I was worried that the passenger might be used to push the vehicle through the rough parts of the track. I was counting on either getting over those rough spots quite easily on horseback or, if possible, taking to the bush and bypassing them completely. A passenger who could help push the car through difficult patches was not part of my plan.

Dunn hotly denied that his passenger would do anything other than give added weight to the vehicle but the bags had me baffled.

"What do you reckon is in those bags?" I whispered to Andy.

Andy gave me a wicked grin and whispered back "There's supposed to be sand in them to stop the back of the car sliding around. Sand is pretty heavy, you know, so I got a young bloke I know to put sawdust in them instead. Mr. Dunn is not carrying the weight he thinks he is! Now let's see how that rear end settles – or doesn't settle."

As to the rules – they were simple. The passenger could not help push the car and the first one over the finishing line wins. By the time we lined up for the start, quite a large crowd had gathered to watch the fun and place a few bets, of course! People were still trying to get a bet on when the starter's gun went off. We were away.

As I expected, Dunn took off on the flat country leaving me behind. By the time we started to climb the mountain, I was well behind. I reckoned the mountain would slow the car down and the horse would soon peg it back once we hit those steep climbs and rough sections of the road – or should I say track? Besides, I had not ridden in this country for years without learning quite a few short cuts – shortcuts that would come in

---

224   There are several versions of this race. This is a compilation of these tales.

very handy on that race if you happened to be on horseback. Remember, I was not obliged to take the same track as Dunn.

At one stage, Ajax[225] and I left the road to clamber up quite a steep slope. I stopped the horse to give him a spell and spotted Dunn and his friend on the road a fair bit below where I was. Sure enough, the passenger was pushing. Of course he was! I would have done the same thing in his shoes.

Well, to cut a long story short, Ajax and I won at a canter although I must admit that Dunn was not as far behind me as I had expected them to be. By the time we got back to the base of the mountain, Andy was gleefully collecting his winnings. Of course, in a small place like that, it did not take long for the tale to have everybody talking about what had happened about the bags of sand/sawdust to get around. Perhaps Andy's mate had told a few of his mates and suggested they put a bet on me. In any event, it did not take long for for the gossip to be flying around the countryside. There were nearly as many versions of the race as there were people. I thought perhaps people might be a bit wild about it but on the whole, they seemed to think it a huge joke. I wonder if Mr. Dunn found out about the trick that had been played on him and if he did, how did he take it?

I seem to remember that it was not long after that that Andy decided to move on. I was quite disappointed because we had a nice little thing going there with the cattle. Perhaps he felt we had been pushing our luck a bit hard with the cattle duffing and it was a good idea to quit while we were ahead. I do not know, maybe he was right. Anyway, he went. I must say I did miss him with his bright ideas (that quite often landed us in strife) and his great sense of humour.

In a way it was good because it left me free to do what I wanted. We had built up a nice little bush telegraph system which kept us informed of

---

225   Research has failed to provide the names of horses Jessie had in Widden Valley. I have given this horse the name of Ajax although it may have been something entirely different. DM

likely cattle movements and also of what the police were doing.[226] Some of the locals were not sympathetic to me but I had a small group of young blokes who would ride with me when some herd proved too much for one person to handle. So I had my 'gang' and settled down to run things my own way. I liked that, not having someone telling me what to do, I mean.

During this time, I really built myself a reputation. If anything went missing then I had taken it! I seemed to have been able to be in two or three places at the one time. That would have been very handy to me, if it had been true. I must admit I was guilty as charged in many of the things I got accused of but definitely not all.

It is quite interesting that quite a few of my neighbours quite liked me. Probably this was because I was careful not to steal too much from them. The Simpsons, for example, would close gates after me if I left them open during one of my night ventures to pick up a few 'stray' cattle.

That was when I started some of the stories about how ferocious I was. I did not mind being friendly with my neighbours, but I did not want too many people just dropping in on me. That could be very dangerous if I had stolen cattle or horses in the yard. Someone told me that Charlie George was so scared of me that he moved into Kandos![227] I am pretty sure that he dobbed me into the coppers once but I was not as bent on revenge as he suggested.

After Andy sold Thalgoona (or its lease) and moved away, I was left with no place to stay, except Hector's of course, but Florrie only put up with me there so I did not feel very welcome. Of course, there was my cave

---

226 There are some pretty wild tales about Jessie even today. However, there can be no doubt that cattle and horses were not the only things she stole. DM

227 Charlie George certainly feared Jessie. It is said that she suspected him of dobbing her in to the police but there is no proof of this. Whatever the cause, Charlie certainly feared Jessie and admitted that he would pull the blankets over his head if he heard her and/or her gang riding past his hut. It is even said that he moved into Kandos until after her death in 1936.

146

but I did not want the location of that known and, besides, it was too hard to get to for anything other than a hideout. I loved Widden Valley and still longed to get some land there. When I saw that there was land there for lease I decided to see what I could get. For once, I got lucky. There was a very nice piece of land along Emu Creek which appealed to me. By then I knew that I could afford the lease fee because I still had a nice little bankroll tucked away in my secret place. No. It was definitely not in the cave!

Once I had that sorted out — and boy! did it take time! — I set about building myself a hut. I found a very nice peach tree growing near the creek and, for want of a better place decided to build my hut there. It was pretty rough at first. It only had a dirt floor and a corrugated chimney with a stone hearth in front of it. I managed to get an iron bedstead and a table and a couple of chairs. I was comfortable enough and I did not have to worry about too much housework.[228]

Young Ken would slip away to visit me. It was not long before we were great mates. I knew Florrie frowned on any contact between her children and me so I did not encourage young Ken — who now had the nickname of Snowy — to visit me too often. Some of my neighbours — Andy Brown and Bremmer Morrison, for example — helped me with the building of the hut. With all that help it was not long before I was as snug as a bug in a rug in my little hut. To celebrate, I planted roses out the front of the hut. When they bloomed it looked very homey and smelled just heavenly.

My biggest problem was the winters. It can get very cold here in winter, even getting snow. Me and my friends built a sort of barn to house my horses and their tack and the sulky I had bought. That stash of money came in very handy then. For my hut, well, in addition to the old bed, table and chairs I had an old fuel stove although I liked to cook outdoors. Such things as blankets, crockery and knives and forks I bought although

---

[228] Once again I rely on Jenifer and Cliff Ellis's description of the remains of Jessie's hut to build a picture of what it was like in the 1930s.

I tried to steal them before parting up with my hard earned cash. We had built a solid fireplace complete with chimney so I could get warm in the winters.[229]

Once I had all this completed, I started looking around for cattle that I could steal and then sell on. My days with Fitz had made me known to many of the dealers who did not look too closely at who really owned the cattle and horses I was selling. Even so, I preferred to alter the brands if I could and sell them through the proper saleyards.

---

[229] Jessie's hut burned down when a grass fire went through the valley. What little remains now is on private property and not open to the public.

CHAPTER EIGHT

HOME ON THE RANGES

Life was good in those days. Now I had the lease on the land and had built my hut I felt that at long last I had roots in this lovely valley, especially after the roving life I had led. I did not actually own the land, but I did have a lease from the Government. Crown land it was called. There was plenty of land in Widden Valley which could be leased by anyone, provided they came up with the fee, of course[230]. Trust the Government to want their share. I was terribly proud when I realised that I was the first person to hold a lease on this particular piece of land, which made it all the more special to me and I held it in my own name all by myself. There it was on the Government papers for all to see – Elizabeth Jessie Hickman.[231]

I was running pretty low on money after I had paid the Government fees and bought some odds and ends for the hut, so I increased the amount of cattle duffing I was doing. I didn't really want to give up the duffing business completely anyway, because I had to build up my hidden nest egg somehow. I knew that there would be a rainy day when I would

---

230   The Land & Property Management Authority
231   The Land & Property Management Authority

probably need the support of a lawyer and they do not come cheap. It was from here that I also started to build up the legend of me being such a blood thirsty person.[232]

Yes, it was hard work keeping the farm going as well as keeping the cattle business going. Also, I had to look after my own horses. I did love them, but although they were dependent on me in many ways, I depended on them too. I could never have carried on the cattle business without good reliable horses. You could say they were the life blood of the business. I think I gave them more care than I did the hut. But then, I always was a rotten housekeeper.

Most country people know how to handle a gun and I was an above average shot. Even as a small child I knew how to use a gun as well as look after it. That is the way it is with country children. Add to that the fact that while I was with Martini's, Billy Waite would give me a few tips. Billy was never a stage shooter but he was a first class shot.

The result was that I rarely missed what I was aiming at. I played on that, telling some pretty tall stories about how good I really was. My idea was to make people in the district – especially those I did not like – very wary of me. I told some pretty tall stories, believe me.

My accuracy with the gun had another good point. There were plenty of animals around that cooked up well in a stew – particularly rabbits – so there was no need for me to go hungry though sometimes I did long for a nice juicy steak or a mutton stew or even a couple of lamb chops. Not only was I able to feed myself but, if I had a good bag of rabbits, I would share them with some of the poorer families in the area. Believe

---

[232] Most of the stories in the following chapters are based on oral history. However, it has been possible to verify some, particularly details of Jessie's 1928 trial. Wherever possible I have given references but must warn readers that most of these tales carry a caveat as to their accuracy.DM

me, large families were the order of the day, then.[233] I suppose they still are to a certain extent.

As I said earlier, I was very lucky to have some good neighbours. Of course, they did a little cattle duffing on the side too, particularly if they came across some unbranded cattle. It really was a case of finders keepers then. Even the well-to-do farmers were involved to a certain degree although I think they would die rather than admit it.

I have mentioned my good neighbours but there were friends that I had outside the valley too. Of course, there were Hector and Florrie in Kandos but I was really thinking more of Gertie Wilson.[234]

Gertie had a farm in Baerami. She has had it tough during her lifetime and we struck up a friendship when I would drive cattle past her farm on my way to Denman to sell them. Gertie lost her husband[235] during the Great War and was faced with running her farm and raising her seven children.[236] Like so many other women in the same position, she set about her very busy life.

We became real good friends, so good in fact that a lot of people thought we were sisters! How we laughed about that! I never could figure out how that story got about although I never did anything to set the record straight then. Perhaps it was because we were both women who did not have a man in their life.

Having said that though, it did puzzle me why she never remarried after her husband was killed in the war. That is what widows were expected to do back then – after all Gertie had a good farm to bring to

---

[233] Refer Jack Drake's comments at the start of this book.
[234] New South Wales Birth Registration 17396/1878
[235] William Wilson, New South Wales Marriage Registration 7743/1896. The family moved to Baerami in 1910.
[236] Elizabeth A 1897; George F 1898; Leslie L 1900; Gertrude N 1903; Stanley W 1905; Hunter P1907; Bessie 1910.

the marriage.[237] Perhaps all those children frightened the men off![238] She made a real go of her farm too, through sheer hard work and I came to admire her a lot. She even bought another farm in the Baerami area and ran both of them with the help of her family. She really was a great woman.[239]

Except for those occasions when things got either of us down, both Gertie and I were pretty happy with our lot. Ours was not a life of luxury but that was not all that important. Look at what we had. Each had her own property to work. Of course, after her family grew up, some moved out and the girls married and went off with their husbands. However, a few stayed on the farm to help her keep it going.[240]

After I got my hut fixed up, I had time to enjoy the beauty of the country around Emu Creek. Oh, it was isolated and rugged in Widden Valley, but that did not bother me. There was so much to see and to observe. The colours that flooded the valley at sunrise and sunset were something to see! The golden light that would bring out the different shades of green in the trees; the reddish brown of the cliff faces; the magic of a spider's web turned into a delicate pattern of diamonds by the dew; the fairyland that appeared on a moonlit night. I loved it all.

Every season had its flowers that would erupt suddenly to form a magic perfumed carpet which lured one to just sit and dream. Even the leaves of the trees, plants and grasses provided such a delicate background of greens for the bountiful floral display. My goodness, I am going all poetic! All I am trying to say is that it is a beautiful place despite the isolation and rugged nature of the country.

---

237 Ellis I *Voices From There To Here* Alladin Publishing 2001
238 Ellis I *Voices From There To Here Alladin Publishing 2001*
239 Ellis I *Voices From There To Here* Alladin Publishing 2001
240 Ellis I *Voices From There To Here* Alladin Publishing 2001

On a more practical note, there was plenty of water in the creeks that ran through the country side. Emu Creek, although hemmed in by cliffs and mountains, had some good farmland to offer settlers in the area. In general, there was plenty of pasture for the farm animals despite the droughts that are the curse of the Australian farmer. Still, they were to be expected and we managed to get through them.

I must mention something really funny that happened after I got my hut finished. I had an old square stove that I fed with cut sapling logs. Someone or other told me about something that saved a lot of time and work cutting up the saplings. I simply poked one end of the sapling into the firebox and left the rest of it resting on a chair-back. As the log burnt I just kept pushing in the log.

One time I asked a friend to stay at the hut while I was away. I think I was taking some cattle to market. Anyway, I left a note that read "Don't bother to saw logs for the stove. Just use the chair wood at the back." Nice and simple. When I got back I found a note saying "There was no chair wood at the back, only log saplings. I expect you meant the old chairs at the front, on the porch, so I used them." The atmosphere in the hut turned blue! I did eventually get some new chairs for the front.[241]

Between Emu Creek and Bylong River was a well-known cave on the Bylong side of the mountains. This was not my little hideout cave but the livery cave I mentioned earlier that Andy Black would hide cattle there when we were moving the stock around. It gave us a nice snug place to camp overnight and even offered shelter for our horses. On the walls were drawings of two horses along with some scribblings that had accumulated over the years. Local legend has it that Captain Starlight and his gang used it during the 1870s. I do not know about that. The

---

[241]   This tale was told to Jim McJannett by a one time circus clown. Jim says his name was "Warren".

names of Marsden brothers[242] are scribbled on the walls and it is claimed that they were in Starlight's gang. I have heard people talking about a family called Marsden who actually lived in the area somewhere around the turn of the century. The boys in that family were said to have been bushrangers but if that is so I do not see how they could have been members of Starlight's gang. Now, I come to think about it though, wasn't Starlight just a made-up character in one of Rolf Boldrewood's books?[243]

This cave was always known locally as the Livery Cave because it was such a good place to rest cattle. I used it a lot when I was moving cattle about. It is no use stealing cattle if you cannot sell them and they need to be in good condition to bring a good price. I could not sell my cattle at the same town all the time either so I had to drive them some distances to reach some of the different towns in the district. That was why I liked to rest them at the Livery Cave.

I liked particularly Denman as another town to sell my cattle. I could sell horses there too but it was the cattle that sold well. Most times I would try to make a private sale where the buyers were not too fussy about who the previous owner was. Butchers especially were usually keen to pick up some cheap meat which would bring them a good profit in their shops, but there were almost always people on the lookout for a sound horse too, so I sold quite a few of them too.

---

[242] The Marsden family lived in the area at the end of the nineteenth century and early twentieth. Local legend has it that the Marsdens were part of Starlight's gang of bushrangers. As Starlight was a fictional character created by Thomas A Browne (Rolf Boldrewood) and is based on four real bushrangers namely Captain Midnight (Thomas Smith), Captain Moonlight (Andrew George Scott), Frank Gardiner and Henry Readford. Frank Pearson is said to be the real Captain Starlight but he never came within hundreds of kilometres of Widden Valley.

[243] T A Brown (pen name Rolf Boldrewood) created Captain Starlight basing his character on the real bushrangers

The hard part of this was finding the right people to approach. I did not want to get myself into trouble by offering stolen cattle to someone who would dob me in to the coppers. Another reason I liked going to Denman was because I could drop in and see Gertie, maybe even stay a day or two with her and help out.

That reminds me of a day I was in Denman and the horse I was riding was suddenly spooked by something or other and started bucking like a maniac. I think even Bobs would have been impressed by this nags effort. Anyway, I rode him bucking like crazy all the way down the main street of Denman.

It caused such a fuss that the ride even got in the paper. I think I can still remember the actual wording of the item. It said, "The ride caused such a stir in the town, not because of the display of superb horsemanship, but because of the profane language of the rider!" I must have really outdid myself.[244]

My so-called gang was a bit of a joke, really. True, I did get quite a bit of help from the young blokes of the area, but they usually only helped me out when I was moving stock from their holding pen to a town for sale. It was no fun taking the lads through those mountains with the trails so narrow and very dangerous. It was even worse in the dark so I had to be careful about the lads who did help me.

I would say that I was alone rather than lonely on my farm. I even encouraged some pretty tall tales about myself in order to keep unwelcome guests away. Some of these tales were true enough, but some were wildly exaggerated. You know how these things happen. Kandos and Rylstone were pretty small places and everyone seemed to know everyone else's business. Let us imagine that I told some tale about my ability with a gun then followed up with some wild tale about how I shot someone or other. Pure fiction, of course! The person I told it to goes away and tells

---

[244]   The story came from Cliff Ellis whose father actually witnessed Jessie's wild ride.

it to a member of the family or a friend and before you know where you are, I have shot up a town or murdered several people!

I remember one story that did the rounds that said I had belted one of the farmers over the head with a branch from a tree, knocking him out. While he was out cold, I was supposed to have stolen the cattle he was moving up the mountain. Charlie, his name was, came to with a nasty gash on his head, but managed to make it home on the horse that I had very kindly left for him. I had even tethered it to a tree to wait for him to recover. His wife reckoned that I had attacked her husband and never had a good word to say for me after that.[245]

Another story had me riding a horse over a cliff into the river. I cannot remember doing anything like that because I really think I have too much love and respect for my horses to treat one of them like that. Such a leap would have been very dangerous for both of us, particularly if there were underwater rocks around there. Perhaps if the coppers were chasing me, perhaps even shooting at me, I might attempt the jump, but I cannot remember ever doing anything like that. Maybe it was just one of my stories come home to roost; maybe someone had been seeing too many movies![246]

Of course, there were many tales about my escapes from the police. I am supposed to have escaped from trains, disappeared through toilet windows, vanished like a ghost into the night, escaped naked when surprised by the police while I was having a cooling dip in a creek and many other disappearing stunts. The one about riding naked through the bush is a scream. It seems that I was taking a refreshing bathe in a mountain pool when the coppers turned up. They are supposed to have got between where I was in the water and where my clothes were but when I saw them I

---

245 The story as told by Shirley Tunnicliffe
246 Pat Studdy-Clift tells a similar story in her book *The Lady Bushranger* but it is also a story told by many of the residents of Kandos/Rylstone. No documentation has been found to support the tale so I consider it to be oral history only. DM

scrambled out of the water, jumped on my horse and rode off into the bush stark naked! Now I ask you! Even the coppers would have had the sense to get between me and the horse! In that case, even if I had managed to get my clothes on I still would not have stood a chance of escaping without the horse. The coppers would simply have ridden me down!

I really did do some of the things I was accused of but a lot were just stories that grew up around me. I did not try to deny or contradict them because they helped make people wary of me. Another good point about them was that I found them really funny when they got back to me.

Once I had a couple of the young blokes in my gang tell the coppers that possums were being illegally poisoned up in the mountains. This was against the law so the police had to go and investigate. While they were away on a wild goose chase, others of us slipped into town and stole the cattle which were being held in the police yard. You can imagine that the coppers did not like that one little bit when they rode back onto town! Wow, did they get a rough time with so many residents jeering at them. Yeah, I remember that one all right. I always did like a good practical joke, particularly at the expense of the coppers.[247]

There was one tale that I liked in particular. There was this dingo which was cunning, destructive and so hard to catch that it was given the name of "Mother Hickman". Two out of three is not bad. I do not think I was destructive but cunning and hard to catch? Yep, I'll take that as a compliment.[248]

There was another thing that the people heartily disapproved of. When I built my hut and the stable for the horses, I went back to wearing trousers

---

[247] Again, Pat Studdy-Clift tells a similar story in her book *The Lady Bushranger* but it also remains oral history. Nevertheless, it is a good tale. Is it possible that these are the cattle reported stolen by Mr. Mills in 1926?

[248] This story was kindly passed on to me by Pat Studdy-Clift after the publishing of her book *The Lady Bushranger*.

again. I had often worn them in Martini's because they gave me more freedom to move about when I was working with the animals. I did not think anyone would worry what I wore up here in the mountains, but it appears that I was wrong.

I was sometimes the victim of theft, too, believe it or not. I remember I discovered that someone was taking the chaff I had for the horses but what really annoyed me was that I had no idea who was doing it! Then one day I walked into the stable only to find a bloke called Bob Dawson at the open chaff box. I jumped to the conclusion that he was the thief of the chaff I had for my horses.

"What the hell do you think you're doing?" I yelled at him. He jumped about six feet in the air and took off like a startled rabbit. I must have been right about him pinching the chaff because it stopped disappearing from then on. Also from then on, Bob avoided me like the plague. Poor man died soon after that, but the big surprise was that his real name was Bob Ball and he had a wife in England! Probably had some kids too if the truth be known. Funny how you remember things like that.[249]

My happy life in Widden Valley went on until sometime in 1926 when a bloke named James Mills lodged a complaint against me claiming I had stolen five cows and a calf and driven them fifty miles to my farm. Maybe I did but I was never going to admit it.

I learned later that the police had called on Ben in Sydney to see if he knew where I was.[250] Well, he didn't of course, but he did not like having the coppers on his doorstep asking questions about me. Off Ben went to see Mum at her home in 88 City Road, Darlington, where she was living under the name of Mrs. Vaughan. Good old Mum said she had not seen me for months and had no idea where I was.

---

249 As told by John Rayner
250 New South Wales Police Gazettes 1926 Pages 629 and 694; 1927 Page 54; 1928 Page 322

It must have been November that the local coppers caught up with me on Nullo Mountain. At this time, Andy Brown was my neighbour on the other side of Emu Creek and would sometimes drop in for a cuppa and a chat. Andy was very unhappy with my cattle stealing and was always trying to talk me into giving it up. Fat chance! I was puzzled though because Andy seemed to be very wary of coppers. Perhaps he had a past that he did not want anyone to know about.[251]

This particular day, we were sitting outside enjoying a cuppa and good old chinwag when a couple of coppers and a Mr. Mills rode up. True to type, Andy sort of just faded away over the creek, leaving me to deal with the coppers.[252]

By this time, it was getting late in the afternoon but the coppers kept on asking questions about Mr Mills' cows and being a real pain in the neck. They wasted so much time that the shadows were closing in on the valley making it seem like dusk. The coppers and Mr Mills wanted to take a look at my cows but by the time they realised how dark it was getting, it was too late for them to do this. So they decided to check out the cows the next day. That was fine with me until they chained me to the bed! Happy that I was safely chained to the bed, all of the dopes settled down for a good night's sleep, leaving nobody to keep an eye on me. The fools should have known better. A little dismantling of the bed soon got the chain free although it was fairly hard keeping the chain from rattling too much. Once free, all I had to do was slip away into the night and get the chain off later with an axe.[253]

That did it. I was on the run from the police who had taken out a warrant for my arrest. It was not long before Roy Halpin and Allan Doyle Willis

---

[251] New South Wales Divorce Records 1472/1927

[252] New South Wales Divorce Records 1472/1927

[253] The police certainly questioned Jessie in November, 1926 and confirmation of the interview appears in the Mudgee Guardian May 10, 1928. However, research has failed to find any support for the claim that she was chained to a bed in 1926 although chaining her to a fence in 1928 was admitted by the police at her trial in May, 1928

had told the police that I had stolen cattle from them too. Hell, all of them could have easily spared those animals but no, they had to turn me into an outlaw! Now I would probably finish up going to gaol if the coppers caught up with me. Then the real game of hide and seek began. I did enjoy the next couple of years so much. It was a real pleasure to take the Micky out of the coppers.[254]

I had plenty of escapes from the police, too, over the years. Mother Nature was a real good friend of mine. I would say I had to go to the toilet which was usually a pretty rough affair. Then I would lock the door or jam it shut, as the case may be, and then either climb out the window or scrape a way under or through a wall. I would be well into the bush before the coppers realised that something was wrong.

Once, I remember, I was in custody on a train with two coppers guarding me. Mother Nature called (or so I said) and they let me lock myself into the dunny. I disappeared off leaving the copper guarding an empty dunny! I got away with this caper quite a bit until they woke up to me and a visit was no longer really a private thing, if you know what I mean![255]

I got into many a tight spot, but I had learned so much about the area from Andy Black that I was able to disappear into the mountains or valleys. Of course, Widden Valley was pretty remote from the towns so I was able to return to my farm quite often and stay there for quite a while without the coppers checking the place out. If they did come on the scene, I would nip out and scuttle up to my cave and hideout there for a while. They must have thought that Andy Brown was looking after the place for me.

If I was driving cattle for sale, it was much harder, of course, but then again, I knew the hidden trails like the back of my hand so I could choose the best and safest one to follow. They were all dangerous when it came to driving the cattle, but one has to take risks if you want to steal cattle.

---

254   New South Wales Police Gazette 1926 Pages 629 and 694

255   The story as told by John Rayner, son of Jean Rayner, friend of Jessie

Once I actually lost some cattle over a cliff and nearly joined them at the bottom myself! That really was a close shave – in more ways than one! The track was narrow, winding through really mountainous country. I do not know what got into me because I could have taken another track but the cops were close on my tail so I must have felt it would be a better idea to take this particular one.

At one really narrow pinch, a couple of head at the front of the small herd went over the edge of the cliff but the worst part was that it spooked my horse and he went over too. I just managed to kick free and throw myself off the horse before he fell. It was a very, very close thing and something I am not likely to forget! I kept rolling away from the edge, then scrambled to my feet, dashed for cover somewhere and finally managed to wedge myself into a narrow cleft in the rocks. A few cattle were still on the track but were frightened by the noise of the falls and some more followed my horse down.

I had to leave the few remaining cows on the track to manage for themselves because the coppers were now really close and I was not game enough to come out of my hiding place. Just like the song "Up came the troopers, one, two, three". Although I was well hidden, I could still hear them talking. Oh, dear! Have you ever desperately wanted to laugh but knew you couldn't because if you did, you would be in real trouble?

Listening to what the coppers were saying, it sounded like they were not sure if I had gone over or not; nor did they know what to do about the few cattle that were still up on the track. They were coppers not drovers and they were on a narrow, dangerous path up the mountain. It was a scream to listen to them arguing about what they should do but eventually they managed to get themselves and the cattle off the mountain in one piece.

I do not know if they came back to see if my body was at the bottom of the cliff but I suppose they did. Anyway, if they did come back they did not find it dead or alive – because I was long gone before they could get the cattle off the mountain then come back to investigate my supposed death.

There was one person who might have been able to lead the coppers to capture me and that was Jimmy McDonald.[256] He was a tracker for the coppers – "black trackers" they were called. Jimmy was an Aboriginal bloke who was one of the best trackers I have ever seen. If he was fair dinkum about tracking me, I knew I really had to watch my step. I was good in the bush but I was not sure I was good enough to fool Jimmy. I know he was well thought of in Rylstone and the coppers certainly thought highly of his tracking skills.

I got on quite well with the district's Aboriginal people so perhaps he had some sympathy for me. I know I sometimes wondered if he deliberately ignored some of the signs I accidentally left behind me.

It was during one of the times that I had to hide out in my cave that I found poor Jimmy out cold on the ground. His horse was a little way off but it was obvious that there had been some sort of accident and Jimmy had fallen quite heavily.

Outlaw or not, I knew I could not just leave Jimmy there like that so I got some water from my waterbag and bathed his face. He did not seem to have anything broken so I thought he must have just banged his head or something. Fortunately, it was not long before he came around but he was very wobbly and certainly would not be fit to ride for a while yet so I decided to stay and see that he was all right.

While he was recovering I went and got his horse for him. He would need that to get back to town or at least to a farm where he could get help. We talked quite a bit on and off. It seems he had been sent out to see if he could find any trace of me. I could not help laughing. There was poor Jimmy being helped by the very person he had been sent to track down. It was enough to make a cat laugh.

---

[256] Jimmy McDonald's obituary Mudgee Guardian

The end of it was that as soon as he felt up to it, I helped him onto his horse to report back to the police station. He gave a funny sort of a wave as he rode off, almost a sort of a salute, in fact. I wonder what he told his bosses when he got back to town.[257] The sensible thing to do was to say that he had found no trace of me and let it go at that. You can be sure that by the time anyone could get back onto my trail again, I would be long gone and probably snug in my cave.

I spent quite a lot of time in my cave. The farm was now too dangerous to stay there for any length of time because the coppers kept dropping by on the off chance they might catch me unawares. That was where my bush telegraph came in. I was kept well informed on police whereabouts by many of the poorer folk who had a lot of sympathy for me. Some of the older kids would sit outside the police station and listen to the talk that was going on inside and then pass it on to me. Because I was so well informed, I could occasionally go back to my farm with no fear of the coppers turning up.

It was about that time that I really started stirring up the gossip about me. I saw it as a good way to frighten people into not going to the police. One of the things I did was to tell young Tindale a story that would be too good for him to keep to himself. I told him that I had killed Fitz.[258] You know, even after all these years, I still hate Fitz. I often wish that I had really killed him so perhaps there was an underlying truth in the tale. Anyway. I made it a good story.

I was sure he would tell his mates who would almost certainly talk about it amongst themselves. One of them would let something slip to his parents and the story would be on its way around everyone. It worked better than I had hoped and soon I was a bloodthirsty murderess. So in a different way, I did get a sort of revenge on Fitz.

---

257   Des Honeysett, grandson of Jimmy McDonald
258   Refer Chapter 5 Note 26

I was still playing catch-me-if-you-can with the coppers when Mum sent me word that Ben had filed for a divorce. Well, I should have expected that I suppose. That would have been in the last months of 1927, I think.[259] I cannot say I was very upset about it. In any event, I did not contest the divorce. To be frank, by the time the divorce came up I had other things to worry about. The coppers had caught up with me and I was under arrest.

It was early May 1928[260] that the coppers caught me at my farm. I had had no warning from my friends that they were anywhere near here so they really caught me on the hop. I was very angry too because I figured that someone must have dobbed me in otherwise the coppers would not have known that I was actually at the farm. They never had before! I never did find out who it was but I did have my suspicions. Let me tell you, I did not go quietly.

I still remember who the coppers were that came that day. Sergeant Buckley from Rylstone, Constable Smith from Wollar and Constable Ingram from Leadville. Jimmy McDonald came trailing behind them looking very unhappy. It was obvious that they had all come out looking for me and that somewhere along the way someone had told them I was at my farm. That was why Jimmy was not in the lead looking for signs. They already knew where they were going.[261]

I happened to be heaping up some hay with a pitchfork when they came riding up. Later they claimed that I had charged them with the pitchfork and screamed, "If you want me, you will have to **** carry me to Rylstone!" Well, the pitchfork was in my hand wasn't it? Of course, I would have turned towards them but charge them with it? Come

259 New South Wales Divorce records 1472/1927

260 Accounts of Jessie's arrest appear in The Mudgee Guardian May 10 and 14 and The Canberra Times on May 15.

261 The Mudgee Guardian May 10 and 14; The Canberra Times May 15

on, I was too surprised to see them there to do more than just gape at them.[262]

I later told the court that the coppers had thrown me to the ground, knelt on me, then handcuffed me to the fence for what seemed like hours. The coppers denied this, as you might expect, but admitted chaining me to the fence.[263]

I could see that Jimmy was not happy with what was happening. The problem then was getting me back to Rylstone to charge me. First up, they thought they would get Mr Dunn to take us all back to Rylstone in his car but he and his family had gone to the Bligh Picnic Races. Eventually, they commandeered a sulky from Major Bullock.[264] The Major was a big bloke but he seemed to be scared silly of me. I heard him ask Sergeant Buckley not to go too far away when he, the Major that is, was near me. What did he think I could do, handcuffed like I was?[265]

I must have hit a nerve when I said they would have to carry me back to Rylstone because they left me handcuffed, but tied me to the back of the sulky and told me to bloody well walk back to Rylstone. They rode in the sulky.[266] On the way, they stopped at the Eames' place where Mrs Eames offered us all a cup of tea. I must admit I was offered a cup too but I would have died rather than join the coppers over a cup of tea. Jimmy and I were left outside in the cold while they trooped inside to the fire and a nice hot cuppa.

---

262   The accusation of Jessie's attack with a pitchfork is recorded in The Mudgee Guardian on May 10, 1928
263   The Mudgee Guardian May 10, 1928
264   Major Charles Cyrus Bullock (1881-1968) Australian born, served in NSW Mounted Rifles in the Boer War (1899-1902) Married Goldie Levy Manhattan in 1906. Served in WW1 in Europe with an English unit.
265   "Brigands of the Bush", Stockman's Hall of Fame Journal, March, 1993
266   This part of Jessie's arrest was told by Des Honeysett, grandson of Jimmy McDonald, who was so appalled at the treatment of Jessie by the police that he recounted the event to his family.

While we waited there, it began to snow lightly and soon after that the Eames family arrived back from the races. It seemed everyone in the district had gone to the races. They were just about frozen too. Jimmy did not say much but anyone could see that he was not happy with the way we were being treated.

The Eames' place was fairly close to Rylstone so the coppers decided to stay with the sulky and not co-opt the Eames' car to finish the trip to Rylstone. Major Bullock was not too happy about this but the coppers made him keep going. So off I plodded to Rylstone. I was so exhausted by the time that we got there that I barely had the strength to swallow some warm food and drink before collapsing into a bunk in the cell.[267]

I appeared in court before Mr H. H. Farrington on May 9, 1928, at Rylstone.[268] Mills, Halpin and Willis said they had identified their cows way back in 1926 and that they were the cows seized by the coppers. Allan Willis added that he had seen his cow in the police yard. As was only to be expected, the coppers told their own version of my arrest and I told mine. It did not make much difference because, although I was released on bail, I had to appear at the Mudgee Quarter Sessions on August 28. Still I was out of gaol and it felt just great.

I decided to stay on the farm and while I was there I got to thinking that it might be a good idea to get myself a good lawyer. I had my little nest egg salted away for just such an emergency and this was an emergency if ever there was one. So I did the thing in style. I was represented by Mr. Dovey who had been instructed by Mr R P Hickson.[269]

---

[267] This part of the story is told by Ian Buckley in "Brigands of the Bush", *Stockman's Hall of Fame Journal*, March, 1993.

[268] New South Wales Police Gazette September 12, 1928 Page 583

[269] The Mudgee Guardian May 10, 1928. Mr Dovey became a well-known name in legal circles.

My defence was simple. The cattle were on Nullo Mountain and had mixed with my herd and I did not know they were there. Who regularly checks every head of cattle on their property for strays? Of course, Mr Mills' cattle would have had to stray about fifty miles, which is quite a step, but cattle have been known to travel further than that. One smarty in the court said, "Yeah! Particularly when someone is driving them!"[270]

I noticed that there were a couple of people on the jury who were my friends and felt sorry for them being put in such a position, but I hoped they would remember our friendship and take a lenient view. After all, nobody is very fussy about who owned what when it came to branding time. They just slammed their own brand on anything that was still unbranded.[271]

It took just one hour for the jury to decide. You can imagine my relief when the verdict was "Not guilty!"[272] I was free to go back to my farm and live there and the cops could not touch me. It felt just great.

[270] The 'smarty' was Constable Smith. The Mudgee Guardian May 10, 1028
[271] Refer Jack Drake's comments.
[272] New South Wales Police Gazette September 12, 1928 Page 583

CHAPTER NINE

LAST DAYS

This trial and all the worry that came with it had driven any thought of the divorce from my mind. Not that I had any intention of contesting it because I thought I was well out of the marriage anyway. Still it came as rather a shock when I got a letter from Mum in November, 1928, saying that the divorce had been granted, but Ben had to apply for it to become absolute. I had thought it would be all over and done with once the divorce was granted. It turns out that Ben had to wait for six months before he could apply for the divorce to be made absolute so we had to wait until May, 1929. I was still stuck in this marriage I never really wanted.[273]

When May came around I wrote to the Registrar of Divorce[274] to check if Ben had applied for the decree absolute. I got a letter back telling me that as of May 28, 1929, no applications had been made.[275]

So I still did not know if I was divorced or not.

---

[273] Divorce 1472.1927 Registrar of Divorce letter dated October 29, 1928
[274] Jess's letter to Registrar of Divorce dated May 23, 1929
[275] Registrar of Divorce letter dated may 28, 1929

Oh well, it did not really matter. I decided to keep the name of Hickman and just settle down on the farm. Young Ken was getting older now and would often come around to visit me. I really did enjoy those visits. We would just sit and talk and I would tell him about my days with Martinis and perhaps some of the more lurid tales of my cattle duffing days.

That was something else I had to decide. What was I going to do about my cattle duffing? The years seemed to be slipping away much faster as time went by and I had to admit my health was not what it had been. This thing in my head was giving me some really bad headaches too. If a headache struck out of the blue, as they often did, it made those dangerous tracks even more difficult for me to try to drive cattle over, particularly at night. Who knew what would happen if I blacked out? Chances were that I would be what went over the cliff this time. Come to think of it, the way I feel sometimes these days, that might not be such a bad thing.

I knew the coppers were keeping a close eye on me as well. It all added up that I really needed to scale down my operations if I wanted to stay alive and out of gaol. This gave me more time to sit around the hut and talk to Ken – and others – about the old days.

Kenneth Hugh Hunt (Snowy) and his friend Reg Kupke.
Photo courtesy of John and Dorothy North.

I still had a fair bit of money hidden in my nest egg so I could manage quite comfortably for quite some time. Still, an unbranded stray calf or cow was very tempting so, needless to say, some still found their way into a saleyard or even a cooking pot occasionally.

I often rode over to Gertie and we would enjoy a great old chinwag but even that started to get a bit much for me. She was still a good friend but going over that mountain was getting harder and harder.

Wally was another who would take the trouble to come into Widden Valley for a chat. He would come riding up the valley, knowing a warm welcome was waiting for him. Occasionally he would stay overnight but not often. He would tell me scraps of news about the people we had known during our days with the travelling shows. He told me that Jack Daly had passed away sometime around 1922, but he did not know where. I was sorry to hear that. Jack was a real character as well as being a great roughrider.

Another time, his news was that Ben had found someone else. He said it was not Kitty but that he seemed very happy with her. I think he said her name was Sylvia[276]. When I come to think about it, we were such an ill-matched couple that I wonder why he was so keen to marry me? Oh, well, young and silly, I guess.

What I really wished I could do was to turn back the clock and go back to the roughriding days with Mart, Jewl and the others! You know, I think I loved Mart more than any other man in my life. Not in a physical sense but purely as a friend, a sort of kindred spirit and someone I could trust and respect. He was old enough to be my father and how I wished he had been instead of that useless sod that sired me.

About that time, I made a very disturbing discovery. My friends told me that I had started doing some very odd things – things that I usually

---

[276] Silvetta Madlene Merry Father:Frank Mother: Mary

could not remember doing[277]. Even now I do not recall them and have to rely on others to tell me what happened or what terrible or silly thing I did. Evidently, one of my favourite tricks was to hitch the horse to the sulky and take off on a wild ride over some pretty awful tracks. I would drive that poor animal until it was nearly on its last legs and I was exhausted. I think I was more worried about my horse's welfare than my own.

A really strange thing happened last year. I got a letter from the Registrar of Divorce referring to my letter of May 11, 1935.[278] As far as I can remember, I never wrote such a letter to them. That shook me up quite a bit.

However, the Registrar told me that the decree absolute had been granted in my divorce from Ben on June 4, 1929. I had been a free woman for six years and never knew it. Nobody had bothered to tell me.

I could not work out the next bit of the letter at all. I must have said something about wanting to marry again because I was told that I would have to produce a Certificate of Dissolution before being able to remarry. I could get this Certificate from the Registrar of Divorce for the sum of 2/6d. (two shillings and six pence)[279]. Who on earth did they think I was going to marry here?

When I came out of these black periods I did not remember what I had been doing or where I had been. And that is a very frightening thing, let me tell you.

Often, during those times, Jimmy McDonald or one of his mates would get me back to their place and look after me until I came out

---

[277]   Col Ribaux et alia

[278]   It is worth noting that Jessie's handwriting in this letter indicates that it has deteriorated significantly to that in her letter of May 23, 1929, leading to the assumption that her brain tumour was seriously affecting her motor skills.

[279]   25ᶜ in current currency.

of my black spell. It was probably for the best that I stayed with them because I think both my horse and I needed a good rest before making it back home. Jimmy and his mates were real good blokes, friends to be proud of.

So my failing health slowly forced me into a much quieter way of life. I am definitely getting weaker and weaker and quite enjoy just sitting in the sun and thinking back to the good days with Mart, Jewl and the others.

Duncan Hector Kenneth in later life. Photo courtesy of John and Dorothy North.

However, because these black spells and headaches are getting more frequent, a lot of people are starting to think that I am crazy. After getting that letter from the Registrar of Divorce last year, I cannot help thinking they may be right! Even Hector and Florrie are worried and want me to get help from a doctor. In my opinion the time for a doctor has passed – if a doctor could ever have helped me anyway.

The other day, Jimmy dropped in for a cuppa and a bit of a chat. He is a good man, is Jimmy – and a good friend. He could not stay long but I knew he was just checking up on how I was doing – as friends do.

After a while he looked at me so sadly then said, "You are going to die soon, Missy[280]." He said it as calmly as if he was just saying I was going to Sydney or somewhere like that but he looked so glum.

I nodded, "Yeah, Jimmy, I know. And you know what? I shall be glad to go. I am so tired – so very tired. The headaches are really bad now so it will be good not to have to put up with them anymore. Still it would be nice to see my roses again. It is almost spring now, but if I don't last that long, that will be just fine. I think I would like to be buried down by the creek. Perhaps something can be arranged, but it doesn't really matter, because I will be somewhere else by then anyway. There will just be this bag of bones to get rid of."

Jimmy got up, walked over to me and put his hand on my head for a second. "I'll call in again soon, Missy," he said. He mounted his horse, waved and headed down the track. As I watched him ride off, I wondered if I would see him again. Probably not. Goodbye, my friend.

No, I am not morbid. I am just a tired, sick, not-so-very-old lady. I have had a varied life of happiness and sorrow but I have lived free. The biggest mistake I made was marrying Ben. For that I am sorry. Wherever he is

---

280   As told to me by Des Honeysett, grandson of Jimmy McDonald, "Missy" was Jimmy's name for Jess.

now I hope he has forgotten me and found happiness with his Sylvia. I still think he really should have married Kitty, you know, but that is something else that it is too late for now. Dear Kitty. How I hope that she has found happiness with Arundel and Hedley.

Hedley. I would like to see him and his family, but it is too late for that, too. Jean, another true and faithful friend, has kept me up to date on what has been happening in his life. I wish I had met his wife, Gladys, and held my baby grand-daughter. Dianne would be over one year old now because her birthday is in March. They gave her a rather strange name – Dianne but it is not pronounced Die-ann as you would expect. Jean says Gladys chose the French way of saying Diane because she had a French doctor for her confinement. Whatever. It comes out as Dee-arn. Figure that one out!

I guess I am sort of saying my goodbyes here. I hope these pages get to the people concerned and that they think of me in a kindly way. It is my belief that I was not born to be a wife or mother. Perhaps the travelling show fostered this in me. Who knows? Now I am tied to this hut by ill-health, but it will soon be over and I shall roam free somewhere in the next world.

The other day who should walk in but Mart! I just looked up and there he was standing in the doorway with a big smile on his face. It was so exciting to see him and I just flew into his arms for a big hug. We talked about the old days for a while, then he moved on to the important thing he had come to say. He said he had come especially to talk something over with me.

"This is it, Jess," he said. "We are going to go north to that lovely warm weather of Queensland. North Queensland as you like it so much. No more of this cold weather down here. We may even decide to join up with some show somewhere. What do you think of that?"

"Oh, Mart", I cried. "Just being together again is as much as I can deal with now. But it does sound wonderful to be getting away from this cold, miserable weather. When do we go?"

"I have a few things to do, but I shall come back for you soon. Just make sure you are ready when I do come. I shouldn't take long, so be quick! When I get back we will just go." With that he kissed me on the forehead and, as he went out of the door, gave me that cheeky wave of his hand that I knew so well. Oh, I am so happy I hardly know what I am doing![281]

*   *   *

I cannot believe that I have written those last paragraphs! Poor Mart has been in his grave now for nearly thirty years. How could I have written such rubbish? Wishful thinking, I suppose. Either that or this wretched thing in my head has had me dreaming of him. Never mind, it was a good dream.

Dear Mart, it will not be long now! Wait for me…

---

[281] Wally Craven told of this meeting with Jess. He said Jessie was "young again".

CHAPTER TEN

A PAUPER'S GRAVE

Jessie died a lonely death, with no family by her bedside, mourners to grieve at her graveside or flowers to mark her passing. She did share her grave with a child buried in the first decade of the twentieth century and a man who was buried only a few weeks before she was buried there. As it was a pauper's grave, there was of course, no headstone to mark those who lay there in their eternal rest.[282] That "something" in Jessie's head was a brain tumour, probably a glioma, which slowly sapped her life from her. Her behaviour became more erratic as time went by. A comparison of her handwriting in a letter dated May 23, 1929[283] and a letter she wrote dated May 11, 1935,[284] shows a marked decline in the clarity of her writing.

---

[282] Records of Sandgate Cemetery, Newcastle
[283] New South Wales Divorce Records 1470/1927
[284] New South Wales Divorce Records 1470/1927

Site of Jessie's grave at Sandgate Cemetery, Newcastle, is indicated by a cross. She shares her grave with a child buried in the first decade of the twentieth century and a man buried there a few weeks before Jessie died. Photo courtesy of Newcastle Historical Society.

The earliest records of her admission to hospital indicate that she was taken to Brentwood Hospital, Muswellbrook, by a Mr. R Simpson.[285] Research reveals that there were two Mr R Simpsons, Royden J and George Rex (known as Rex). It was probably Roy who took her to Muswellbrook as Rex was an accountant living in Denman.[286] Research has failed to reveal details of her condition or how Mr. Simpson became a Good Samaritan and drove her to Brentwood Hospital. Mr. Simpson told authorities at Brentwood that Peter Hunt was her brother and Mrs. Wilson was her sister, both statements being incorrect.[287]

Jessie was placed in the care of a Dr. G. S. Abbot at Brentwood Hospital. Dr Abbot treated her for a week with little success, then decided to refer her to the Newcastle Psychiatric Reception House for observation. In his referral letter he describes her condition as "very restless, refuses to answer questions, has not been violent." An unsubstantiated claim is that Jessie just lay in her bed rocking her head from side to side and did not seem to understand questions that were put to her. She arrived at the Reception House, in a coma, at 9.50am on September 15, 1936. In his report on her death the Medical Superintendent describes her condition as "R facial paresis, inequality of her pupils and a right side Babinski."[288] She obviously had some grave cerebral condition. She gradually got worse and died." She died at 5.10pm of the same day.[289]

All this seems quite straight forward. However, due to the misinformation supplied by Mr Simpson about Jessie's relatives, hospital authorities decided to hand the matter over to the police in an effort to find Jessie's

---

285   New South Wales Medical Records 4028/1936
286   C & J Ellis, Scone
287   New South Wales Medical Records 4028/1936
288   The Babinki Reflex (extensor plantar reflex). This occurs when the big toe flexes towards the top of the foot and the other toes fan out after the sole of the foot has been stroked. This is normal in younger children but abnormal after the age of two. Above the age of two, Babinski's reflex indicates damage to the nerve paths connecting the spinal cord to the brain (the corticospinal tract)
289   New South Wales Medical Records 4028/1936

family. Despite this, Hector wrote a letter to the hospital on September 16, 1936, seeking information about Jessie.[290] It is obvious that he received the news of her death within twenty four hours of it occurring. In reply to Hector's letter, he was told in a letter from the Medical Superintendent that the matter had been referred to the police.[291]

Interestingly enough, William Norris, who had a property near Jessie's, identified her body on September 17.[292] This is verified by his sworn statement dated September 28,1936. A post mortem was conducted on Jessie's body with the result being "a very extensive cerebral tumour, probably a glioma, in the left front and pereital regions. The diagnosis has been made with great confidence before death."[293]

September 19, 1936 Jessie was buried at Sandgate Cemetery, Newcastle,[294] in a pauper's grave already containing a child and a male.

On September 21, Hector was sent a letter by the staff of the Newcastle Psychiatric Hospital advising him that his letter had been referred to the police who had taken over Jessie's affairs. The reason for placing the matter in the hands of the police was that Jessie's relatives could not be found. This is most interesting because both Hector and William Norris, her neighbour, knew of her death within twenty four hours.[295]

An inquest into her death was held on September 29 and the coroner found that she died of natural causes. Although it has often been

[290] Research could not trace a copy of this letter but reference is made to it in a letter from the Medical Superintendent of the Newcastle Psychiatric Reception House dated September 21, 1936.

[291] Medical Superintendent's letter dated September 21, 1936

[292] Affidavit of Death dated September 28, 1936 and signed by William Norris of Emu Creek, Kerrabee.

[293] New South Wales Medical Records 4028/1936

[294] New South Wales Death Registration 16080/1936

[295] New South Wales Medical Records 4028/1936 and Affidavit of Death signed by William Norris

mentioned that she died of pneumonia, there is no mention of that in any of the documents relating to her death. Put simply, she died of a brain tumour.[296]

At first glance, it would seem that authorities had been hasty in consigning her body to a pauper's grave. Surprisingly, the firm of funeral directors who handled Jessie's burial[297] are still operating in Newcastle and supplied information about burials in the 1930s. Their records no longer extend back that far but they were able to clarify one problem. Patients who passed away in mental hospitals during those years were frequently buried in pauper's graves, because there was simply nobody willing to accept responsibility for the body. Either the patient had no close family or the family refused to accept responsibility for the burial. Therefore, it is not unreasonable to assume that, under these circumstances, the authorities would only make a token effort to locate a patient's family as past experience had taught them that it would probably be a waste of time and money.

As one might expect, Jessie died intestate resulting in a probate being required. Her estate[298] totalled £151.17.0 (one hundred and fifty one pounds, seventeen shillings) being Stock & Implements £118.7.0 (one hundred and eighteen pounds seven shillings; leasehold £32.0.0 (thirty two pounds) and furniture £1.10/- (one pound ten shillings).

Why was Jessie consigned to a pauper's grave? Was the family ashamed that Jessie had died in a Mental Hospital, hence the rumour that she died of pneumonia? Was it because they were ashamed of her life duffing cattle and stealing horses? Or was it because they simply could not afford to take her body back to Kandos and bury her there? Australia was still recovering from the Great Depression in 1936 and it is quite possible that no family member could afford to give her a proper burial. We probably will never know the truth now.

---

[296]   A Chiplin, Coroner, Newcastle
[297]   J Meighan, Funeral Director
[298]   Probate 220813 dated May 14,1937

Epilogue

What Became of Them?

BEALE Arthur (aka Arthur Grant)

Jim McJannett tells the following story "I was at Rotorua rodeo in 1963 as a competitor. (I was never any good but it was enjoyable). I got talking to an old bloke as a result of him giving me a few pointers on how I should have ridden a twister of a steer from which I was tossed just before the hooter. I commented on the good ride by a female. "That good?" he said. "You've never seen good riding by a lassie unless you saw Jessie Hunt. But she was before your time. Bareback or saddle, horse, steer or bull, no one could hold a candle to that girl! She was magic! These kids are tame today!" The 'old bloke' was Arthur Beale who, in later conversation with Jim, would arouse Jim's interest in the life of Jessie and also supply Jim with so much information about Jessie and her days with Martini's.

Arthur advised Jim to get in touch with Wally Craven who also knew much about Jessie's life after the death of Mart. Arthur had worked in Martini's and could supply a great amount of information about Jessie and Kitty. He eventually went back to New Zealand where for some reason, he adopted the name of Grant. He is reported to have gone to the islands north of Australia but nothing is known of him after that.

BEISCHER Charles Theodore

Refer James Hunt

BELLATI Paul

Paul was born in Turin, Italy, the son of Augustus and Katherine Bellati, in 1860. He liked to travel and fetched up in Sydney around the first few years of the 20th Century. He married Christina Nicol on April 27, 1908 when she was eighteen and he was forty eight. The marriage did not last long and resulted in a rather messy divorce in 1920 although it was not made absolute until 1925. In 1923 he was seeking employment in Brisbane as a carpenter. There he claimed to be French but could speak English and Italian. After that little has been found about him, but it appears that he returned to Sydney some time later. He died in Sydney Hospital on February 6, 1937 aged seventy seven. His death registration gives him as a "labourer, old age pensioner".

CRAVEN P Walter (Wally)

On Arthur's suggestion, Jim tried to contact Wally when he, Jim, returned to Australia. Unfortunately, Wally had moved out of the address given to Jim and it took Jim some years to track him down – even then it was the result of a co-incidence.

Wally had kept in touch with Jessie on and off over the years, but little is known of what became of him after Jessie's death.

FITZGERALD John

Much has been made of the supposed murder of Fitz by Jessie in about 1920. A diligent search for a death certificate which meets the details of the oral history about Fitz's murder has been made – even to the extent of purchasing copies of numerous death certificates – but with no success. The details have always indicated the age of the dead person was incorrect; the time of death did not match with the oral history; the location of where the person died did not tally. There was always something that did not fit.

During their conversations in the 1960s, Wally told Jim that Arthur had bought a horse from Fitz in the year that The Trump won the Melbourne Cup. There was considerable doubt as to whether the horse was Fitz's to sell. Arthur was livid about the whole affair. Little research is required to confirm that The Trump won the Cup in 1937, the year AFTER Jessie died in 1936. If Fitz was alive in 1937, then Jessie most certainly did not kill him! If Fitz was murdered at a later date, then it certainly was not Jessie who did the deed.

HICKMAN Benjamin Walter

Ben was born September 17, 1882 at Bletchington, Oxfordshire, England, the sixth of nine children born to Thomas Hickman, agricultural labourer, road labourer and farm worker, and Mary Anne Bazeley. When Mary Anne died in 1895, Ben was fortunate enough to be accepted onto the Training Ship *Mercury*. In fact, the *Mercury* was a barque known as *Illova* purchased by philanthropist, Charles Hoare and renamed *Mercury*. Under that name it was used as a training ship (TS) and provided sea training for the sons of impoverished parents prior to them becoming sailors in either the Royal or Merchant Navy.

His service in the Royal Navy took him to many places including Sydney, Australia, where he met Jessie Hunt, roughrider extraordinaire. As already told, theirs was a stormy relationship which ended in divorce in 1928. At some time, either before or after their divorce, Ben met Silvia Cole (nee Merry). Actually, her correct first name was Silvetta but she was known as Silvia.

TS Mercury was a ship used for training young boys fifteen and over for service in the Royal Navy or the Royal Merchant Navy. Photo courtesy of the TS Mercury Old Boys Association, England.

Ben continued in his employment at Prouds Ltd. until he retired, with Silvia, to the Entrance in coastal New South Wales. He is said to have told siblings that he did not find happiness with his first wife (Jessie), but he did with his second (Silvia). Ben continued to live at the Entrance to a ripe old age of eighty eight. A stalwart of the RSL there, he died on New Years Day, 1971. He was cremated at the Northern Suburbs Crematorium on January 4, 1971 and his ashes scattered in the grounds there.

HICKMAN Silvetta (Silvia)

Silvetta was born in 1895 to Frank and Mary Merry. Although the records of her early life are sketchy, she has left us a diary which gives a little information about herself and Ben. The diary contains some financial records and some sort of a code. Is it possible that Ben did a little SP betting in 1929? In addition to this it tells a little about herself.

From this invaluable little book we learn that Silvia was born in Silverton, Broken Hill, on November 6, 1884. She married her first husband when she was twenty nine. They separated but no divorce was ever sought. Could this be another case of bigamy or did Ben and she just live together until such time as she could legally marry Ben - that is, following the death of her first husband? The diary remains frustratingly silent on this point.

Silvia died January 8, 1978 at the ripe old age of ninety three.

HUNT Florence (nee Carney)

Florence was born in Tuena near Burraga. Her parents were Patrick and Catherine Carney. She married Duncan Hector Kenneth Hunt, Jessie's brother, at Brewarrina on June 21, 1913. Their children were Kenneth Archibald Hugh, Florence Jessie (known as Jessie), Jack Patrick,

Margaret Katherine (Kit) and Elise Silvia. A family story is that the last born daughter, Daphne May, was really the daughter of Jessie (father unknown). Descendants of Daphne have made enquiries in an effort to prove or disprove this story but, sadly, it looks like remaining a mystery. With the people concerned now dead, there is little hope of getting a solution to this. Daphne's birth certificate does not name Jessie as her mother, but an illegitimate birth was often covered up with false information in the birth registration. Whether Daphne was Hedley's half-sister or his cousin is unknown at this time. Florence died in 1981.

HUNT Duncan Hector Kenneth

Hector was a hard worker and raised his family conscientiously. Although his wife, Florence, did not approve of Jessie, Hector (often called Ken) did what he could to help Jessie from time to time. However, with a large family to care for this was often very little. His cottage still stands in Kandos to this day. He died in Rylstone November 16, 1959.

HUNT Kenneth Archibald Hugh (aka Young Ken or Snowy)

Young Ken was born at Stockyard Creek, Buckburraga, on April 18, 1914, some thirteen months after the birth of Hedley. When Hector and Florence settled in Rylstone and Kandos, many people believed that he was the son of Jessie, in fact some still do. However, this is one family tale that is quite incorrect. Young Ken married Dorothy Francis Jackson in 1940 and they had three children, a son and two daughters. Young Ken died on April 12, 1990.

HUNT James

As revealed in the Prologue of this book, James' real name was Charles Theodore Beischer. After he left the sea, he turned to mining and finished up in the Macquarie Shire. Rumour has it that he spent some time near Kandos where Jessie visited him. It is well established that Jess detested him and it is inconceivable that she visited him even if he did live in Kandos. James died on June 24, 1939 and his occupation is stated on his death certificate as Old Age Pensioner, Labourer. The cause of death was pneumonia and septic injuries to legs. He died in the Wellington Hospital and is buried in an unmarked grave in the Church of England Cemetery, Wellington.

HUNT Susan Ann

Susan's place of birth is variously given as Tuena and Thompson's Creek, Burraga. She was the daughter of Duncan and Matilda (nee Warren) McIntyre and one of thirteen children. She was illiterate but insisted that her children go to school to learn to read and write. She had relatives who lived in Bankstown which was a community of farmers in those days. Susan often visited them and it was there that Jessie learned to ride a horse. Susan never really deserted Jessie as research reveals that she kept in contact with Jessie over the years. Even as late as 1926 there is evidence of Jessie visiting her mother in City Road, Darlington.

Susan died in Royal Prince Alfred Hospital, Camperdown, Sydney on September 21, 1939, thus outliving Jessie by three years. Her cause of death was hypostatic pneumonia and congestive heart failure. She was buried on September 23, 1939, in the Roman Catholic Cemetery, Rookwood.

PRYOR Arundel Rignold Ernest

Born in Nabiac NSW on October 23, 1889, Arundel (aka Run, Arthur) came to Sydney to join the Australian Imperial Forces in World War 1. There he met Christina Bellati who became the love of his life. Unfortunately, she was just not interested in Arundel. Arundel wrote to her regularly when he went overseas with the Australian Light Horse.

From Egypt he sent her many gifts including a moonstone necklace and ear-rings set. These became a family heirloom. When the final break came between Christina and Ben, he seized his opportunity and he and Christina married. He never formally adopted Hedley, something that was to cause a major rift in the family years later. However, he did provide well for Christina and Hedley, eventually taking Hedley as an apprentice in his plumbing business.

During World War 2, Arundel joined the CCC (Civil Construction Corp) and was sent to Townsville to participate in building a hospital near Rising Sun. Always an entrepreneur, Arundel started many ventures to make quick money, most of which failed dismally. It was his plumbing business that gave him the start to try these ideas. When Christina died in 1952, Arundel was like a lost soul. He drifted around the country for ten years before suffering a heart attack in January, 1962. He died in Prince Henry Hospital, La Perouse, on February 7, 1962 and is buried with Christina in the Presbyterian Section of Botany Cemetery.

PRYOR Christina Margaret
(nee Nicol and aka Glen Christina Pryor)

Christina was heart-broken when Ben Hickman deserted her to marry Jessie. She married Arundel (whom she always called 'Run') on November 26, 1920, only weeks before Jessie and Ben married on December 11, 1920. It was probably the reaction of a 'woman scorned' but she built a happy life for herself with Arundel and Hedley. As told earlier, she was very proud of the fact that she was one of the earliest women to get a driver's licence and she kept that spirit of adventure right through her life. During World War 2, she was a warden in the NES (National Emergency Service), sallying forth with her tin hat on her head, her knapsack over her shoulder and a masked torch in her hand.

In Matraville, she was often called 'Nurse" because she would always be ready to help those in need, particularly the sick. In both Matraville and Mascot there were large Chinese gardens. The Chinese people were treated very badly by the general population in those days. They lived in miserable huts made of corrugated iron sheets (if they were lucky) which were ovens in the summer and freezers in the winter. In winter they suffered dreadfully from colds, flu, bronchitis etc. Christina would present herself armed with red flannel vests that she made herself, Vicks Vapour Rub and a whole armoury of treatments for the various ailments. Nobody in need of help was turned away empty handed.

A year or so after the end of World War 2, she went legally blind from retinal dystrophy or macular degeneration as it is called now. Still undaunted she would travel into Sydney's CBD to do her shopping taking Dianne with her as a guide whenever possible. Of course, she could no longer drive a car, so had to use public transport. To cross a road at the lights, she would simply walk when everyone else walked; stop if other people stopped.

In late 1951 she was diagnosed with cancer. In those days that was a virtual death sentence. Few people recovered from most forms of cancer. She died at home in 173 Beauchamp Road, Matraville on July 11, 1952 and is buried in the Presbyterian Section of Botany Cemetery.

PRYOR Hedley Rupert (Hickman Bellati)

Hedley was only seven years old when Christina and Arundel married in 1920. He received a good schooling and did his trade apprenticeship with Arundel. Very athletically inclined, Hedley enjoyed all forms of sport and was a very good story teller as well. This was probably his Hunt blood showing through. In the early 1930s he met and married a pretty blonde eighteen year old named Gladys Simpson. Two years later their first child was born, a daughter whom they named Dianne. Gladys insisted that this be pronounced Dee-arn in the French manner.

During the 1930s Hedley pursued his sporting activities; playing Rugby League Football for Botany Boys Club; social tennis and even riding in the Goulburn to Sydney bicycle race in a couple of years. His second daughter, Pamela, was born in Paddington Women's Hospital in 1942. With the advent of World War 2, he enlisted in the RAAF as a LAC (Leading Air Craftsman). He was discharged "Medically Unfit for Further Service" July 13, 1945. The war left him a sick man suffering from sudden blackouts two or three times a week. He was virtually unemployable. Times were very hard for the small family and it is hard to know how they would have managed without the help of Christina and Arundel.

It took several years and a car accident to reduce the frequency and severity of these blackouts. He then started his own plumbing business, going on to become an estimator, a Justice of the Peace and Secretary of the Australian Estimators' Association.

Gladys died in 1985 and, just like Arundel, he drifted around trying to find a meaning to life without her. Hedley died of cancer in St George Hospital, Kogarah, Sydney on April 23, 1996 aged eighty three. He and Gladys are buried together in the Independent Section of Nowra Cemetery, NSW.

RAYNER Jane (nee Nicol, aka Jean)

Jane was Christina's older sister. Jane was born in Kiama in 1886 and married John Henry Rayner in 1906. They had a large family: Jean 1908; Hilda Mary Rose (Fay) 1909; Nona Alice 1911; Keziah (Kay) Edna 1915; Rachel (Ray) 1917; Pearl 1919; John William (1922) and Beryl (1924). Jane suffered from diabetes and her health was poor. Despite this she was a staunch friend to both Christina and Jessie during their wilder days. It was she who kept Jessie informed about Hedley, although Jessie may not have been very interested. Jane died in 1958 and her death was registered at Rockdale, Sydney. Following her death, her husband, John, burnt Jessie's letters that Jane had kept thus depriving the family and, indeed, Australia of a good insight into Jessie's character and her life in the bush.

RYAN Jullia (nee Kelsen or Kelson)

Julia was born in Victoria around 1877, the daughter of Lauritz and Maren Sophia Kelson and sister to the famed trick bicycle rider, Mena Val. Both girls were involved in show business as Julia did a song and dance act under the name of Miss Devine. Julia joined up with Martini when they were both with Lance Skuthorp's show, leaving it together when Martini formed his own travelling buckjumping show in 1901. They toured up and down the east coast of Australia until Martini's death in 1907. Julia was shattered at losing Martini, but tried to keep the show going. It proved too much for her by herself and she married James Ryan, reputed to be a sportsman from Brisbane in 1909. James is often referred to as Mick Ryan, but the marriage registration shows his name as James. This attempt to save the show was not successful and they sold Martini's Buckjumping Show in 1910. Julia died in 1937 at Burwood, Sydney.

WILSON Gertrude (nee Brown)

Gertrude became a close friend of Jessie's, so much so that many thought they were sisters! Gertrude Maria Brown was born in Scone in 1875, so she was considerably older than Jessie. She married William J. Wilson in 1896 in Muswellbrook where they had their family. As often happened during World War 1, William enlisted and went off to fight, but did not return. Gertrude was faced with providing for her young family, a problem she solved by raising the money to buy a small farm at Baerami. The farm flourished and Gertrude was able to extend her acres by purchasing a further acreage containing a house, dairy buildings, piggery and sheds. Gertrude died in Denman Hospital in 1946 at the age of seventy. The cause of death is stated as being a burst appendix following a misdiagnosis by her doctor.

ACKNOWLEDGEMENTS

During Christmas week 2002, a long lost cousin came to visit me and reveal the story of my father's birth. John Rayner was not sure whether he should tell me this tale or let sleeping dogs lie. His wife, Elaine, told him to go with his heart. What a wise lady! This book is the result of what John told me and, at the time of writing, nearly eleven years of research. Although John turned my world upside down, I am grateful that he and Elaine had the courage to tell me something that would send me on a long journey into the past.

John told me of a book that had been written about my grandmother, Elizabeth Jessie Hickman. When I realised that she was now known as the 'lady bushranger' I was stunned. That book, *The Lady Bushranger*, written by Pat Studdy Clift told me much about my grandmother. However, I did find anomalies in it that I decided to research. Pat also gave me the address of a researcher, Jim McJannett, who lived in Northern Queensland, who had done some research on Jessie. This was a very generous professional gesture and I thank Pat for that.

In Jim I found a dedicated researcher of Australian history, a friend and a mentor over the coming years. His generosity in making his previous research available to me, his experience in research and constant help have made this book possible. He took a raw beginner in research (I did not even know how to get a birth certificate) and encouraged and taught me so much about family research. Words fail to express my gratitude.

Of course, I must thank my long suffering husband, Garry, for putting up with me during the past eleven years. He has endured my frustration when some problem could not be resolved, when some obscure photo or newspaper article turned my theories on their head or when just setting this all on computer made me so tired and irritable. He has even chauffeured me around the state chasing up some information. He is so very supportive.

To attempt to individually name all the people who have helped one way and another in this research would still result in some being omitted. So to avoid hurting feelings, I will only say that you know who you are and what you have done to make this book a reality and my heartfelt thanks go to you.

Finally, I would like to thank the businesses and government departments for their help in chasing up information about Jessie, her family and friends. Many, such as the faceless people at Ask a Librarian, have gone to great trouble to help me find some minor detail to verify some theory, or otherwise. I would like to name these organisations as they are not that many and to extend my thanks to them.

Army Museum, Victoria Barracks, Sydney, NSW
Arnotts Biscuits
Australian War Memorial, Canberra ACT, (Jane Peek)
Bland Shire Library, West Wyalong, NSW
Richard Briggs and Snowy White, TS *Mercury* Old Boys Association, England
Vanadia Sandon Humphries, Bridport, England
Historic Houses Trust of NSW, Sydney (Megan Martin)
Newcastle Historical Society Inc., Newcastle NSW
New South Wales Police Archives, Sydney NSW (Laraine Tate)
Sandgate Cemetery Trust, Newcastle NSW
Stockmen's Hall of Fame, Longreach, Queensland
Wyalong Family History Group Inc., Wyalong NSW

BIBLIOGRAPHY

The Convict Ships Charles Bateson, published by A H & A W Reed, Sydney

Ships Deserters J Melton

Annals of Burraga Kevin Toole

The Lady Bushranger Pat Studdy Clift, Hesperian Press, Perth WA

Golden Rule Days Senior Citizens of Denman District

Little Big Top Fred Ward

Time Means Tucker H P (Duke) Tritton

Robbery Under Arms Rolf Boldrewood

The Horse Tamer Jack Pollard

The Silver Road Mark St.Leon, Butterfly Books

Thorpe McConville's Wild Australia, Ray McConville

Australian Cowboys, Roughriders and Rodeos, Jenny Hicks, Harper Collins Publishers Pty Ltd

Bushrangers – Heroes or Villains Edgar F Penzig, Tranter Enterprises

Starlight's Trail James Cowan

Voices From There To Here Ian Ellis

The Man Who Was Starlight Patrick McCarthy, Allen & Unwin

Australian Bushrangers Sasha Molitisz

Stand and Deliver – 100 Australian Bushrangers Allan M Nixon, Lothian Books

Crime and Punishment Allan Sharpe, Kingsclear Books

The Wild Colonial Boys, Frank Clune 1958 Angus & Robertson

Soldier Boy, Anthony Hill, Penguin Books

The Western Front 1916-1917 John Laffin, Time Life Magazines (Aust) Pty Ltd

Breaker Morant – A Backblock Bard Ted Robl

INDEX

Hickman, Silvetta (nee Merry), 173, 189, 191

Hickman, Thomas, 189

Hickson, R. P., 166

HMS *Argylshire*, 109

HMS *Powerful*, 79

HMS *Rupert*, 89

HMS *Tamar*, xxiv

HMS *Terrible*, 77

HMS *Yiringa*, 119

Hoskins, George, 45

Hudson, Mrs. *See* Hickman, Elizabeth Jessie

Hunt, Daphne May, 138, 192

Hunt, Duncan Hector Kenneth, 176, 191

Hunt, Elizabeth Jessie, iii, xv, 2, 5, 143, 149, 199

Hunt, Elsie Sylvia, 138

Hunt, Florence (nee Carney), 137, 191

Hunt, Florence Jessie, 138, 191

Hunt, Jack Patrick, 138, 191

Hunt, James, xxvi, 4, 10, 15, 188

Hunt, Kenneth Archibald Hugh, 137, 191-92

Hunt, Margaret Katherine, 138, 192

Hunt, Robert, 4

Hunt, Susan Ann (nee McIntyre), xxii, 4, 193

Hunton, Jemima, xxii

Hyland's Vice-regal Circus, 14

I

Indigo Creek, Victoria, 25

Ingram, Constable, 164

J

James, Phillip, 95

Jonas, William, 81

K

Kandos, New South Wales, 132, 134-35, 139, 142, 146, 151, 155-56, 185, 192-93

Kelly, Edward (Ned), xiv, 25, 81

Kelsen/Kelson, Julia Charlotte, 197

Kelsen/Kelson, Lauritz, 24, 197

Kelsen/Kelson, Maria Sophia, 24

Kelsen/Kelson, Wilhelmina (Mena Val), 23-24, 35

Kemp, Miss. *See* Gould, Mary Ann

Kemp, Professor. *See* Daly, Patrick

Kenmore Mental Asylum, 27

Kennedy, Harry, 61

Kiama, New South Wales, 71, 106, 196

Kirribilli, Sydney, 107

Kitty. *See* Nicol, Christina Margaret

Kogarah Bay, Sydney, 85

Kurrajong, New South Wales, 31

L

Lee, Billy, 81

Livery Cave, 153-54

Lloyd, Edward (Ned), 81

Long Bay Penitentiary, 95

Lytton's Australian Roughriders, 43, 47, 80, 201

M

Marchand, Olympe, 121, 125

Margaret Nicol, ix

Martini, James (Mart), 2, 33, 35-42, 44-46, 49, 51-56, 59-61, 63-65, 72-75, 79, 81, 83, 85, 173, 178-79

Martini's Buckjumpers, 23, 35, 38, 83, 120

Matraville, Sydney, ix, 194-95

McConville, Thorpe, 80-82, 201

McDonald, James, 63, 132, 162-65, 174, 177

McIntyre, Duncan, 4-5, 193

McIntyre, Elizabeth, 119

McIntyre, Matilda (nee Warren), 5

McIntyre, Susan Ann. *See* Susan Hunt

McJannett, Jim, x, xxv, 11, 43, 45, 54, 79, 81, 120-21, 153, 187, 199

Meighan's Funerals, 185

Melbourne Cup, 189

Mills, James Frederick, 158

Morant, Henry Harbord (the Breaker), 14, 43, 202

Moree, New South Wales, 31

Morrison, Bremmer, 139, 147

Morrissey, Jack, 81

Mudgee Guardian, 159, 162, 164-67

Mulligan, Gertrude Bessie. *See* Valdares

Mulligan, James. *See* Valdares

Murray , G. *See* Hickman, Elizabeth Jessie

Muswellbrook, New South Wales, 183, 197

N

Neave, Alfred E., 80, 82

Nelson, Harry, 53

Newcastle Psychiatric Reception House, 183-84

Nicol, Christina Margaret, ix, 194

Nicol, Hilda (nee Smith), 71, 107, 196

Nicol, Jane (aka Jean), 71, 85, 91, 103, 106, 114-15, 124, 127, 160, 178, 196

Nicol, Margaret (nee Love), 71, 106

Nicol, William Alexander, 71, 106

Nicol, William Hamilton Alexander, 107

Norris, William, 184

North Sydney Football Club, 109

Norval (passenger ship), 106

Nott's Sawmill, Armidale, 55

NSW Police Gazette, xxiv, 11, 143, 158, 160, 166-67

Nullo Mountain, xiii-xiv, 134, 139, 159, 167

O

Oaks, 95

Old Devonshire Street Cemetery, Sydney, 50

O'Meara Street, Kogarah, 84

P

Paddington, Sydney, 56, 119, 196

Paisley, Scotland, 106, 124

Parker, Samuel (aka John Fitzgerald), 98

Pascoe, Alfred, 81

Payne, Mrs. *See* Hunt, Elizabeth Jessie

Peelwood, New South Wales, 4

Pentridge Gaol (Melbourne, Victoria), 27

Pollard, John, 11

Port Jackson & Manly Steam Ship Co., 108

Pozieres, France, 110-11

Prendergast, Jack, 44, 59

Proserpine, Queensland, 51

Prouds Ltd., Sydney, 91, 105, 191

Pryor, Arundel Rignold Ernest, 193

Pryor, Glen Christina (nee Nicol), ix, 194

Pryor, Hedley Rupert Hickman Bellati, 89-90, 195

Q

Queenslander, 28, 46

R

Rawson Place, Sydney, 49, 51

Rayner, Jane (aka Jean nee Nicol), 85, 160

Rayner, John Henry, 71, 196